THE AMAZING BOOK OF

♦ ♣ ♥ ♠

BRIDGE

HOW TO MASTER THE ARTS OF THE GREATEST OF CARD GAMES

BRIAN SENIOR

TIGER BOOKS INTERNATIONAL
LONDON

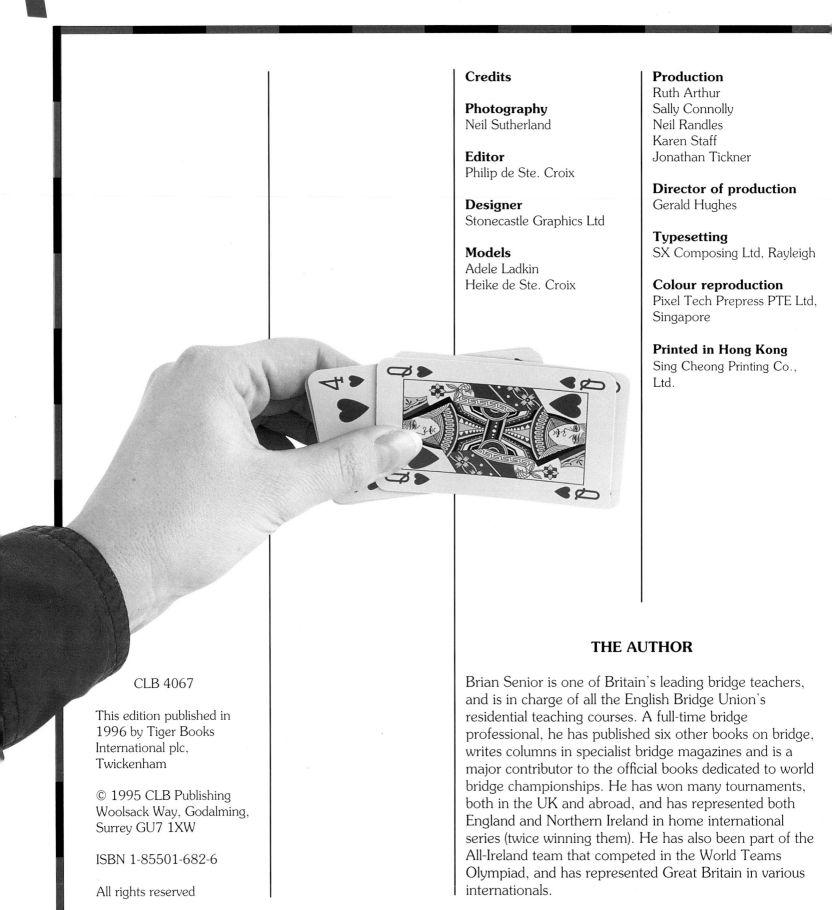

Credits

Photography
Neil Sutherland

Editor
Philip de Ste. Croix

Designer
Stonecastle Graphics Ltd

Models
Adele Ladkin
Heike de Ste. Croix

Production
Ruth Arthur
Sally Connolly
Neil Randles
Karen Staff
Jonathan Tickner

Director of production
Gerald Hughes

Typesetting
SX Composing Ltd, Rayleigh

Colour reproduction
Pixel Tech Prepress PTE Ltd,
Singapore

Printed in Hong Kong
Sing Cheong Printing Co.,
Ltd.

CLB 4067

This edition published in
1996 by Tiger Books
International plc,
Twickenham

© 1995 CLB Publishing
Woolsack Way, Godalming,
Surrey GU7 1XW

ISBN 1-85501-682-6

THE AUTHOR

Brian Senior is one of Britain's leading bridge teachers,
and is in charge of all the English Bridge Union's
residential teaching courses. A full-time bridge
professional, he has published six other books on bridge,
writes columns in specialist bridge magazines and is a
major contributor to the official books dedicated to world
bridge championships. He has won many tournaments,
both in the UK and abroad, and has represented both
England and Northern Ireland in home international
series (twice winning them). He has also been part of the
All-Ireland team that competed in the World Teams
Olympiad, and has represented Great Britain in various
internationals.

INTRODUCTION

Welcome to *The Amazing Book of Bridge*, a book which will introduce you to one of the most fascinating and rewarding games in the world today. Bridge is the king of card games, but it is also much more than that. It is intellectually challenging, yet also of great social benefit.

Bridge is one of the few competitive activities which can be enjoyed by all age groups and in which all age groups can compete effectively against one another. As well as the obvious pleasures of playing the game, bridge can be very helpful in training young minds to think logically yet not just in straight lines, while in one's later years the stimulus it provides can help to keep one mentally sharp.

Bridge also has just the right balance between skill and luck. In what other game can the club player meet the international without the experience being deeply unsatisfactory for one side or the other? In the long term, greater ability will prevail, but in the short term, anyone can beat anyone else. Herein lies one reason for bridge's continuing appeal. Bridge is a game which you can play to whatever level suits you, according to your level of enthusiasm and the time and energy you have available to put into it. If you just want to be able to play at home with friends after dinner, you need only learn the basics, and you will still be in the sizeable majority among bridge players worldwide. If you have a more competitive instinct, there is a whole range of local club, district, national and even international events to aim at and a huge literature on all aspects of the game to help you to achieve your goals.

Bridge is not the easiest of games to learn but I promise you that, however confusing it may seem at first, it is worth persevering. The efforts you put in at the start will be richly rewarded in the years to come.

Most bridge books, especially for beginners, are grey, unattractive looking things which would hardly encourage the undecided to buy and, more importantly, read them. In *The Amazing Book of Bridge*, we have tried to use a different approach. Throughout the book we have made liberal use of full colour photographs, and many examples which would have been given as a black and white diagram elsewhere are portrayed here in colour. Bridge is an exciting and fascinating pursuit and we want this book to help it to capture your imagination.

Bridge is a game in two parts, the auction, then the play. However, the auction will seem much more relevant once you have some grasp of the play section, so in the early stages of the book the order is reversed, i.e. we cover the basic elements of play first. Indeed, the various areas of the game are covered in the order I would choose if I actually had you live in front of me in a beginners' class.

The Amazing Book of Bridge takes you quite a bit further than most beginners' texts. The later sections on both bidding and play are not essential to your enjoyment of the game, but are there for those who would, for example, come back for a course of improvers' lessons a year after the beginners' course had ended.

As for the bidding language itself, it is a considered amalgam of the standard British and American styles, not exactly like either but close enough for the reader easily to be able to make the small adjustments necessary to play with someone brought up in either school.

Bridge is a wonderful game. Enjoy it and good luck to you all.

PART ONE

GETTING STARTED

PREPARING TO PLAY BRIDGE

Bridge is a game for four people, playing as two opposing pairs. The minimum of equipment required to play is simply one complete pack of cards with the jokers removed, though ideally one would use two packs and each of the four players would have their own personal scoresheet and pen (**1**).

The first step in preparing to play a game of bridge is to decide who will play together. You may wish to play in set partnerships, for example with your wife or husband against another couple. If everyone is happy with this arrangement, fine; if not you would **cut** for partners. This is done by someone shuffling the cards, and placing the pack face down on the table. Each player in turn now draws one card from the pack and places it face up on the table in front of them (**2-5**). The players with the two highest cards will play together, as will those with the two lowest.

Before going any further we should look at the ranking order of the cards. In each suit, the ace is the highest card and the two is the lowest (**6**).

There is also a ranking order of the suits, the significance of which will become more apparent later on. The order is (**7**):

Highest ♠ — Spades
  ♡ — Hearts
  ◇ — Diamonds
Lowest ♣ — Clubs

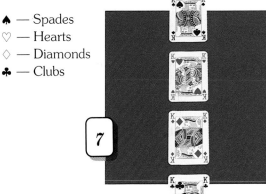

Until you get used to this, a useful memory aid is that the ranking is in alphabetical order.

So let us suppose that the four cards drawn from the pack are (**8**):

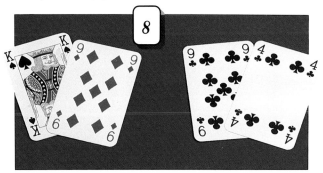

The ♠K is the highest card and whoever drew it will partner the player who drew the ◇9, the ranking order of the suits splitting the tie between the two nines. The player who drew the highest card now has the choice of where to sit and, if two packs of cards are in use, which pack will be used for the first deal. His partner will sit opposite him with his opponents to his right and left. As a form of literary shorthand, the players are described as the four points of the compass as shown below.

North

West   East

South

Suppose that South drew the highest card. The player who drew the second highest card will be her partner so sits North. West will shuffle the pack and pass it to East to cut. This means that East divides the pack in two then puts the bottom part on top of the original top part. South picks up the pack and **deals** out the cards, one at a time in a clockwise direction (**9**) starting with West until all 52 cards have been dealt out, giving each player 13.

While South is dealing, North shuffles the second pack (usually with different coloured backs) and places it to her right, next to West (**10, 11**). This acts as a useful reminder whose deal it is next. When it is time for the next deal, West passes this pack to South to cut, then West deals the cards out while East shuffles

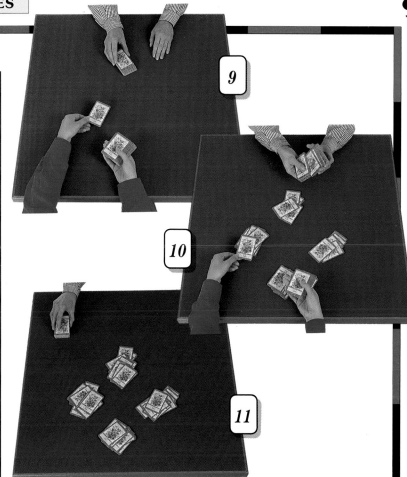

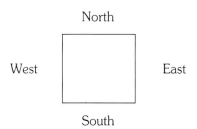

the first pack and places it on his right, next to North, and so on. The sequence of dealing passes clockwise from player to player around the table.

At the end of the deal, each player picks up his or her cards, known as their **hand**, and looks at them but keeps them hidden from the other players. It makes subsequent play easier if you sort your hand into suits and, within each suit, into the ranking order of the cards so that you can see exactly what you have. For example (**12**):

STARTING TO PLAY

Bridge is a game of two parts, the **bidding** and the **play**. The bidding comes first in the course of the game, but to understand its purpose we really need to look first at what happens in the play.

THE PLAY

Each player has 13 cards and plays one to each of 13 **tricks**. A trick is simply a collection of four cards, one from each player. The basic aim of the game is to score as many tricks as you can for your side, though at the end of the bidding, as we shall see later, you will actually have a specific minimum target in mind. As bridge is a partnership game, always remember that it is just as good for your partner to win a trick as it is for you to win it yourself.

The first card played to a trick is known as the **lead**. After it has been made, each player, going clockwise, plays a card to the first trick. Whoever wins one trick leads the first card to the next trick, and so on. Where possible, each player must **follow suit**, that is, play a card of the same suit as that led. Failure to do so when you have a card of the right suit is called a **revoke** and will lead to your being penalized.

Most hands are played with one suit as **trumps**, a sort of master suit which is decided by the bidding. A player who is **void** (has no card left) in the suit led to a trick may play a trump, or **ruff**, and any trump beats any card of an ordinary suit. Alternatively, a player may **discard**, throw away a card in another ordinary suit.

Unless a trump is played, the trick is won by the highest card played of the suit led. Even the two of trumps, however, beats the ace of an ordinary suit. If two trumps are played to a trick, the higher one will win it. A discard can never win a trick.

Sometimes a hand will be played without a trump suit. This is known as playing in **No Trumps**. In this case, if a player has no card left in the suit led, he has no option but to discard.

EXAMPLE TRICKS

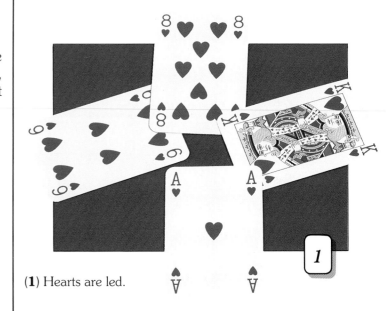

(**1**) Hearts are led.

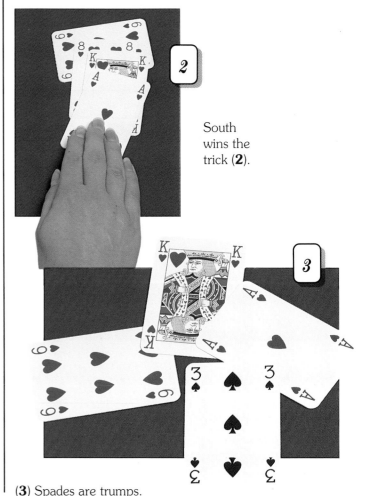

South wins the trick (**2**).

(**3**) Spades are trumps.

Although East played the highest heart, South ruffed so wins the trick (**4**).

(**5**) Spades are trumps.

Though South played the highest card to the trick, it was a discard. East, who ruffed, wins the trick (**6**).

DECLARER, DUMMY AND THE DEFENDERS

The bidding tells us what suit, if any, is to be trumps. It also tells us who will be **declarer**, who **dummy**, and who the **defenders** or **defence**. The declarer is the player who first bid the suit (or no trumps) in which the final bid was made. This final bid tells us in what denomination (suit or No Trumps) the hand is to be played. The player to declarer's left will always make the opening lead, i.e. lead to the first trick. Say that South is to be declarer, then the scene is this:

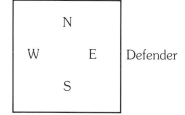

Dummy

Defender and
opening
leader

Declarer

The defenders are sometimes known as declarer's left-hand opponent (here, West) and right-hand opponent (here, East) respectively.

The opening leader makes his lead and dummy now places his hand face up on the table arranged in suits. The trump suit is always placed on dummy's right (on the left as declarer looks at it), so if clubs were trumps dummy might be arranged like this, in four columns facing declarer (**7**). It is normal, though not compulsory, to alternate the red and black suits.

Dummy takes no further part in the play of the hand, declarer selecting the cards to play from both her own hand and from dummy. This enables declarer to use her side's combined assets to the full, though of course she must still only play from each hand in rotation, i.e. from dummy after West's play, from her own hand after East's play.

THE SCORING

At the end of the bidding, or **auction**, declarer has promised to make a minimum number of tricks with her preferred suit, if any, as trumps. As we shall see shortly, that number is six plus the number of the final bid. If she succeeds, she scores points. If she fails, she scores nothing but her opponents score points.

Each denomination has a trick value, as follows:
Clubs and Diamonds: 20 points
Hearts and Spades: 30 points
No Trumps: First trick 40,
subsequent tricks 30 each.

If you bid and make a contract that is worth at least 100 points you score **game**. A **rubber** goes to the first side to make two games and a large bonus is added to their score.

Game can be scored on one deal by bidding and making:

5♣ or 5♢ — 5x20 = 100
4♡ or 4♠ — 4x30 = 120
3NT — 40+(30x2) = 100

It may also be scored in easy steps by making two or more **partscores** – any contract where the trick score comes to less than 100. Unfortunately, if your opponents make a game in the meantime, your partscore will be nullified so far as being a step towards game is concerned.

There are also two types of contract which attract very large bonuses. These are **small slams**, where you contract to make twelve tricks, and **grand slams**, where you need to make all thirteen tricks. Be warned, while those bonuses are very tempting, if you fall even one trick short you will score nothing when you could have chalked up an easy game had you been more cautious.

When you make game but bid only to partscore, you are rewarded for every trick you make, but only the number of tricks you actually bid count towards game. So bidding 2♡ and making ten tricks scores 60 (2x30) towards game and 60 (2x30) extra for the two **overtricks**. If you fail in your contract you score nothing. Instead, your opponents score penalty points.

Before your side has made game in the rubber you are known as **non-vulnerable** and each **undertrick** (trick by which you fall short of your contract) costs 50 points. After you have score a game you are **vulnerable** and each undertrick costs you 100 points. These points do not count towards game.

If an opponent believes he can defeat your contract he may **double** you. He does this by saying "double" when it is his turn to speak in the bidding phase of the game. If he is right, the penalties for failure are increased. If he is wrong and you are successful your trick score is doubled plus you get a small bonus. The doubled trick score counts towards game, the bonus does not. If you have been doubled you are entitled to **redouble**. This increases the scores even more, to twice the doubled trick score and bonus if you are successful, to twice the doubled penalty if you fail.

Finally, you may score points for simply holding **honours**. This means that whether you are declarer, dummy or a defender, if you hold four or five of the top trump honours (AKQJ10) in one hand (**1**) or all four aces in a No Trump contract (**2**), then you score a bonus. This does not count towards game.

Full details of the scoring can be found on page 123.

1

14

2

Below, you can see what a rubber bridge scorecard looks like. Only tricks bid and made go towards game. They are scored below the horizontal line. Everything else is scored above the line. It counts in your final score but not towards game.

	WE	THEY	
TOTALS	990	290	
Bonus for winning a two game rubber	700	200	DEAL 4. You bid 1NT but make only five tricks
	40	30	
DEAL 1. You bid and make 4♠	120		DEAL 2. They bid 2♡ and make nine tricks
DEAL 3. You bid and make 2NT	70	60	
DEAL 5. You bid 3♣ and make eleven tricks	60		

You win the rubber by a margin of 700 points. Usually this is divided by 100 and you say you won a "seven point rubber". This is rounded to the nearest 100, 50 counting as zero.

	WE	THEY	
TOTALS	1740	100	
Bonus for winning three game rubber	500		
Vulnerable small slam bonus	750		
DEAL 4. They bid 4♠ but go one down	100		
DEAL 1. You bid and make 2♠	60	100	DEAL 2. They bid and make 3NT
DEAL 3. You bid and make 3♢	60		
DEAL 5. You bid and make 3♡	90		
DEAL 6. You bid and make 6♠	180		

You win the rubber by 1640 points; a 16 point rubber.

DECLARER PLAY — FIRST THOUGHTS

Declarer has a huge advantage over the defenders. As soon as the opening lead has been made, and before she has to play a card from either her hand or from dummy, she sees all her side's combined assets. Now is the time when the fate of more contracts is decided than any other.

The weak player takes no time at all, grabbing whatever tricks are staring him or her in the face, then looking around to see where more might be found. Often, it is now too late. The thinking player takes a little more time before playing to trick one, trying to make a plan which utilizes the combined assets of her own hand and dummy to the best advantage. It is fair to say that even a bad plan may be better than having no plan at all.

Your contract tells you how many tricks you need to make. 1NT requires seven tricks; 2NT eight tricks; 3NT nine tricks, and so on. Count the number of top tricks you start with in each suit, then take the total away from the number you require for your contract. This tells you how many more tricks you need to find. For example, if you are in 1NT and count five top tricks you know you need two more from somewhere – seven minus five equals two. So how do you count top tricks?

	Declarer	Dummy	Tricks
(i)	A32	654	1
(ii)	A32	K54	2
(iii)	A	K	1
(iv)	AKQ	432	3
(v)	AQ2	K43	3
(vi)	AKQJ10	432	5
(vii)	AKQ32	J104	5
(viii)	AKQJ32	654	6

Notice from (iii) that you can never take more tricks in a suit than you have cards in the longer holding. Also, (iv) and (v) are equivalent. You just make sure that you play one high card and one low card to each trick and you will make the maximum number of tricks available. Finally, in (viii), you might think there are only four sure winners. Think a moment though; your opponents have to follow suit when you cash the four top winners, and as you hold nine cards in your combined hands, there are only four left in the defence's hands. So they will be exhausted of the suit by the time you reach the three and two.

Having counted your tricks, you must plan to take them in the right order. While AQ32 opposite KJ4 gives an easy four tricks; AQ32 opposite KJ is more awkward. One opponent has at least four cards in the suit, so you cannot afford to waste two top cards on the same trick. In the latter case you will need to **unblock** the KJ, then find an entry in another suit to take the AQ at a later stage.

AK2 opposite Q3 creates a similar problem. If you win the first round with the ace or king, you leave K2 opposite Q, an awkward blockage. A good general rule, though you will come across exceptions, is to play the honours from the shorter holding first. Here if you win the first round with the queen you are left with AK opposite 3 – no problem.

TAKING STOCK

It is normal for dummy to be laid out as shown with each suit in a vertical column facing towards declarer. If there is a trump suit, this is placed on dummy's right. The suits are usually placed with alternate colours next to one another, black, red, black, red, but this is not compulsory. Apart from the trump suit, there is no set order for the suits.

Suppose on the example hand (**1**) declarer is in a contract of 6NT. That means she needs to take twelve tricks in No Trumps. By carefully playing one high card and one low to each trick, declarer can make four spades, four hearts, three diamonds and one club – twelve in all. It does not matter what order she takes them in on this particular deal. The only thing she must be careful of is to take all twelve tricks before giving up the lead by, say, playing ace and another club. What would stop the defenders from cashing all the rest of the clubs?

Here (**2**), South plays in 3NT on the lead of the ♣K. She counts three spades, four hearts, one diamond and one club – nine in all – but must be careful not to block either of the major suits. She should win ♣A, carefully unblock the ♡KJ, then play ♠K and ♠5 to dummy. Now she can cash the remaining hearts and spades followed by ◇A.

PLAY SUMMARY BOX												
TRICK												
1	**2**	**3**	**4**	**5**	**6**	**7**	**8**	**9**	**10**	**11**	**12**	**13**
W ♣K	S ♡K	S ♡J	S ♠K	S ♠5	N ♠A	N ♡A	N ♡Q	N ◇6	S ◇2	W ♣Q	W ♣J	W ♣10
N ♣3	W ♡4	W ♡6	W ♠3	W ♠6	E ♣9	E ♡8	E ♡10	E ◇9	W ◇K	N ♣4	N ♣5	N ♣7
E ♣9	N ♡2	N ♡3	N ♠4	N ♠Q	S ♣2	S ♣6	S ♣8	S ◇A	N ◇8	E ♠10	E ◇J	E ◇Q
S ♣A	E ♡5	E ♡7	E ♠2	E ♠8	W ♠7	W ♡9	W ♠J	W ◇7	E ◇10	S ◇3	S ◇4	S ◇5

Each column shows the cards played to that trick with the winning card highlighted – a square box for declarer, a circle for the defence. So, on the first trick, South wins with the ace of clubs, and leads the king of hearts at trick two. Why not make up the full deal with a pack of cards and go through the play trick by trick?

ESTABLISHING EXTRA TRICKS

There are two simple ways of establishing extra tricks. The first one is by knocking out missing high cards. Suppose that you hold:

	Declarer	Dummy
(i)	KQJ	762
(ii)	QJ10	543
(iii)	J1098	6432
(iv)	KJ2	Q76
(v)	Q103	J54
(vi)	J942	10863

In each case, if you were only counting top tricks, ones you could take immediately, you would have to say that the answer was zero, because a defender has the top card in the suit. Yet there are some potential tricks there in each case.

In (i) sacrifice the king to force out the ace and you will establish the queen and the jack as tricks for later. In (ii), sacrifice the queen and jack to force out the ace and king and you establish the ten as a winner. Even in (iii) you can eventually force out the missing high cards to establish one trick for yourself. Although your honour cards are divided, if you look closely you will see that (iv), (v) and (vi) are exactly equivalent to (i), (ii) and (iii) respectively.

LENGTH WINNERS

If we can exhaust our opponents of cards in a suit, any cards we still have left in that suit will be winners.

	Declarer	Dummy
(i)	AK543	762
(ii)	AK43	7652
(iii)	AK32	654
(iv)	A6543	K72
(v)	A543	K762
(vi)	A432	K65

This is not quite a sure thing, in the way that knocking out high cards is, because the missing cards need not be evenly divided between the defenders' hands. Nonetheless, there is a very good chance of exhausting your opponents of cards in each of these suits.

In (i), play ace, king and a third round and if the missing cards are divided 3-2, you will have established two extra tricks. In (ii), play ace, king and a third round and if the missing cards are divided 3-2, you will establish one extra trick. In (iii), you need a 3-3 break, but if you get one the same technique is worth one extra trick.

It is just as effective to **duck** the first round of the suit, playing low from each hand. The defence gets its one trick but when you later cash the ace and king you exhaust them of the suit and can cash your long cards also. Holdings (iv), (v) and (vi) are again identical with (i), (ii) and (iii) respectively.

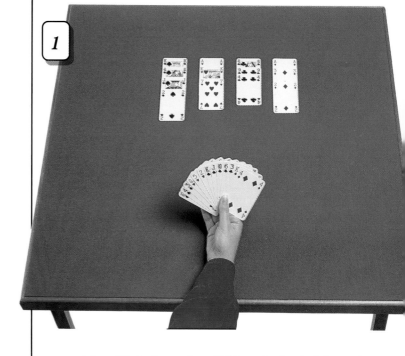

Here (**1**) declarer plays 3NT on the lead of the ♡J. She can count only five top tricks – three hearts and two diamonds – but both clubs and spades offer the chance to establish extra tricks. Declarer should win the ♡A and play the ♣Q and ♣3, then ♣9 and ♣6, and continue until the ace is taken. She is guaranteed four club tricks in return for giving one up. When she regains the lead she can knock out the ♠A in the same way and come to eleven tricks.

Note that all this must be done while declarer is still in control of the red suits. If she cashes her red suit winners then attacks clubs, she establishes winners for the defence and will go down. Try it and see.

STACKING TRICKS

Each side collects its tricks won and stacks them neatly. To ease counting, they are usually stacked alternately vertically and horizontally as shown (**2**).

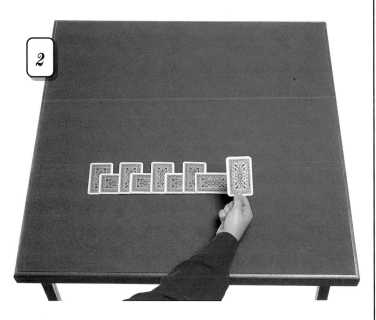

9 tricks won

In hand (**3**) South declares 3NT on the lead of the ♡J. She counts seven top tricks – one spade, three hearts, one diamond and two clubs – so needs two more. The only real hope is a 3-3 club split, establishing two extra length tricks. If declarer played ace, king and a third club she would create the two tricks, but how would she reach them? She must duck the first round of clubs to preserve an entry to the rest of the suit, then comes to nine tricks.

PLAY SUMMARY BOX												
TRICK												
1	**2**	**3**	**4**	**5**	**6**	**7**	**8**	**9**	**10**	**11**	**12**	**13**
W	S	E	S	N	N	N	N	S	S	S	W	W
♡J	♣4	◇10	♣7	♣A	♣8	♣6	♡4	♡K	♠A	◇3	♠K	◇Q
N	W	S	W	E	E	E	E	W	W	W	N	N
♡3	♣2	◇A	♣9	♣J	♡7	♠8	♠9	♡10	♣J	◇J	♠6	♠7
E	N	W	N	S	S	S	S	N	N	N	E	E
♡6	♣5	◇7	♣K	♠3	♠4	♠5	♡A	♡8	♠2	◇5	♡9	◇K
S	E	N	E	W	W	W	W	E	E	E	S	S
♡Q	♣10	◇2	♣3	♣Q	♡2	♡5	♡9	♠10	♠Q	◇8	◇4	◇6

Again, try laying out the full deal using a pack of cards and play it through trick by trick. Then repeat the exercise if declarer plays the ace and king of clubs immediately without first ducking one and see the difference.

THE FINESSE

We have seen two ways of establishing extra tricks. The **finesse** is a third way though there is no guarantee of success. A finesse is an attempt to win a trick with a card which is not currently the highest one out. Take a look at these card combinations.

	Declarer	Dummy
(i)	K2	43
(ii)	AQ	32
(iii)	KQ2	543
(iv)	A32	QJ10
(v)	A32	Q54
(vi)	AQ10	432
(vii)	AJ10	432
(viii)	KJ10	432

What you would like is to win as many tricks and lose as few tricks as possible in each case. Suppose in (i) that you lead the king; whoever has the ace wins it and you make no tricks from the suit. Perhaps you prefer to lead the two? This time the ace does not go up; they win the trick cheaply and save the ace to beat your king next time round. No, your only chance is to lead low from dummy *towards* your king. If the next player holds the ace he has a choice of playing it, in which case you play the two, or playing small, in which case you play the king and it wins. This is only a 50-50 chance, but that is a lot better than no chance at all – which is what all the alternative plays give you.

How should you play examples (ii) to (viii)?

(i) Lead low from dummy and, unless the king appears, finesse the queen. Half the time the king will be where you want it to be and you will have two tricks and no losers.

(iii) Lead low from dummy and, unless the ace appears, play the king. If that wins, play another suit to get back to dummy and lead low towards the queen. This time you always had one trick; half the time you will get two.

(iv) Lead the queen and, if the next hand plays low, play low from hand. If the queen holds, try the jack next. When the king is in front of the ace you have it trapped and make all three tricks.

(v) This time you have no jack and ten to back up the queen so if you lead it, the king will beat it wherever the king is. You should lead low from your hand towards the queen and hope the king is on your left. This is just like example (i) in effect; lead up towards the high card.

(vi) Lead low from dummy and play the ten if the next hand plays low. Whether this wins or loses to the jack, cross back to dummy in another suit and finesse the queen next. If either king or jack is in front of the ace you get a second trick, while if they are both there you get all three tricks.

(vii) Lead from dummy and finesse the ten. Assuming this loses, lead from dummy again when you can and finesse the jack. You are sure to lose to one of the king and queen, but if either or both are in front of the ace you will make a second trick.

(viii) Leading low to the king is wrong, as even when it holds you make only one trick, losing later to both ace and queen. To make two tricks you must finesse against the queen. Lead low to your ten and, if that wins or loses to the ace, cross back to dummy to lead low to your jack. Half the time you will get your second trick.

Due to partner's over-optimism you reach 7NT on this hand (**1**). Can you make it?

You will need some luck. Both the spade and club kings will have to be well placed so you can finesse against them. Win the opening lead and play a club to the ten, a spade to the ten, a club to the jack, a spade to the jack and a club to the queen – of course playing the ace instead, if the king is played in front of it. If all these finesses succeed, you will have a lucky thirteen tricks and a huge slam bonus.

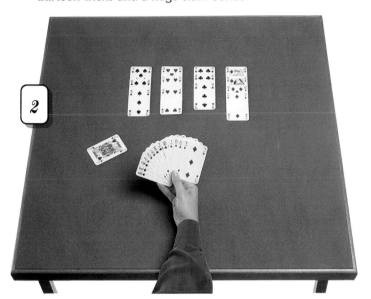

Again (**2**) you have got yourselves a little too high, this time to 5NT on the lead of the ♡J. How should you play? There are six top tricks in the majors so you must find five more. Three can come from diamonds by knocking out the ace and two from clubs, if you are lucky enough to find East with the queen. That will need you to be able to take two club finesses so you must be careful not to waste your dummy entries. Don't cash all the diamonds then take the finesse. How will you get back to dummy to repeat it?

PLAY SUMMARY BOX												
TRICK												
1	**2**	**3**	**4**	**5**	**6**	**7**	**8**	**9**	**10**	**11**	**12**	**13**
W	S	S	N	W	S	W	S	N	S	S	S	S
♡J	◇J	◇3	♣3	♡10	◇6	♡9	◇8	♣4	♣K	♠A	♠K	♠Q
N	W	W	E	N	W	N	W	E	W	W	W	W
♡4	◇5	◇9	♣2	♡5	◇A	♡8	♠2	♣6	♣8	♠5	♠8	♡2
E	N	N	S	E	N	E	N	S	N	N	N	N
♡3	◇2	◇10	♣10	♡6	◇Q	♠4	◇K	♣J	♣7	♠3	♠6	♠7
S	E	E	W	S	E	S	E	W	E	E	E	E
♡Q	◇4	◇7	♣A	♡K	♡7	♡A	♠9	♣5	♣9	♠10	♠J	♣Q

This is how the complete deal looks (**3**).

TRUMPS

All the techniques we have seen for use in No Trumps are equally valid in a trump contract. Possession of a trump suit gives you extra options. The first benefit of a trump suit is that it gives you greater control of the play.

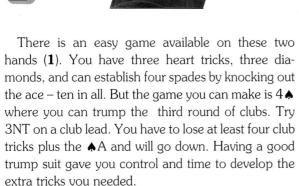

There is an easy game available on these two hands (**1**). You have three heart tricks, three diamonds, and can establish four spades by knocking out the ace – ten in all. But the game you can make is 4♠ where you can trump the third round of clubs. Try 3NT on a club lead. You have to lose at least four club tricks plus the ♠A and will go down. Having a good trump suit gave you control and time to develop the extra tricks you needed.

A second benefit of a good trump suit is that it enables you to establish length tricks in a side suit without having to lose tricks along the way. Look at hand (**2**).

Say a club is led against 4♠. You can win the ace and play ace and king of hearts then ruff a heart. If hearts are 3-3 they are now established and you can draw the missing trumps and cash your hearts. If hearts are 4-2 you simply ruff a club to get back to your hand, ruff another heart and now draw trumps. Again, no problem.

A trump suit can also provide extra tricks even when you do not have a side suit to establish. Consider this hand (**3**).

In 4♡ you have nine top tricks – two spades, five hearts and the two minor suit aces. The surest source of an extra trick is to ruff your third club in dummy. Win the opening lead, play ace and another club and, as soon as you can regain the lead, ruff your club. Now you can draw the missing trumps and take your ten tricks.

THE CROSS-RUFF

Generally speaking, it is only by ruffing with the shorter of declarer and dummy's trump holdings that you create an extra trick. You were probably going to make the long cards in the longer hand eventually anyway.

In the next example (**4**), it looks as though extra tricks are being made by ruffing in both hands, but in fact declarer started with five trump tricks in his own hand. All his three club ruffs did was to give him entries to hand to take the three spade ruffs in dummy; they were the extra tricks which came out of the **cross-ruff**.

There are only nine top tricks in 6♡ but three spade ruffs bring the total to twelve. Win the diamond lead and cash the other top diamond. It is good technique to cash your outside winners before embarking on a cross-ruff just in case a defender gets the chance to discard a diamond while you are cross-ruffing and later ruffs your diamond winner.

Now you are ready for the cross-ruff. Play the ace then ruff a low spade, ace then ruff a low club, then take alternate spade and club ruffs until both suits are exhausted. You will just have two trump winners left to cash at the end and twelve tricks in all.

BIDDING – WHAT'S IT ALL ABOUT?

Having learned a little about the play of the hand, you will be able to recognize the advantage of having a good trump suit. That is where the bidding comes in. Bridge is a partnership game. Your side's best trump suit may not necessarily be the suit in which you happen to hold most cards. It is the best *combined* holding you are after.

During the bidding you and your partner try to exchange information about your hands until one of you is in a position to decide which, if any, trump suit you should choose. Remember also that there are big bonuses available for bidding and making game or slam contracts. Not only must you choose a trump suit, you must also decide how high to bid, whether or not to try for one of those large bonuses. Each bid you make should tell your partner something more about the shape and strength of your hand.

The language of bidding is very limited, being restricted to the following:

- The numbers: 1 to 7
- The suits: clubs, diamonds, hearts, spades, No Trumps
- The words: Pass, Double, Redouble

Like everything in bridge the bidding goes clockwise, starting with the dealer. He may make a positive bid – a number of a suit – or may pass if he has nothing to say at this stage. The bidding continues until there have been three consecutive passes since the last positive bid. When the bidding comes round to you, you may bid, always a higher bid than the last one, or pass. You may double an opposing bid, or may redouble if an opponent has doubled you or your partner. If a doubled or redoubled contract is left in, the number of tricks required to fulfil it is not changed but the points scored by the successful side are dramatically increased.

The bidding is also known as the **auction**. Just as in a real-life auction, you may always pass but if you want to bid over someone else you must outbid them, i.e. make a higher bid. This is important in two ways. Firstly it means that you do not have limitless time in which to describe your hand to partner, because the bidding is getting ever higher. Secondly, you have opponents. Often the auction will become competitive. Their idea of an attractive trump suit is likely to be very different from yours. They will try to outbid you so as to earn the right to choose their preferred trump suit. The currency of the bidding is tricks.

There is a ranking order of the suits, clubs being the lowest:

CLUBS DIAMONDS HEARTS SPADES NO TRUMPS

Lowest ➤ Highest

To outbid somebody you must either bid the same number of a higher ranking suit than theirs or bid a higher number of any suit.

There is considerable skill in judging just how high to keep bidding in a contested auction. Sometimes it can even be right to bid higher even though you know you will fail, i.e. to make a sacrifice bid, because you think the cost will be lower than letting your opponents play in their chosen contract.

The first thing you do on picking up your hand is to assess its strength. The way you bid will reveal to your partner your judgement of its playing potential.

THE BIDDING LADDER

7NT seven No Trumps
7♠ seven spades
7♡ seven hearts
7♢ seven diamonds
7♣ seven clubs
6NT six No Trumps
6♠ six spades
6♡ six hearts
6♢ six diamonds
6♣ six clubs
5NT five No Trumps
5♠ five spades
5♡ five hearts
5♢ five diamonds
5♣ five clubs
4NT four No Trumps
4♠ four spades
4♡ four hearts
4♢ four diamonds
4♣ four clubs
3NT three No Trumps
3♠ three spades
3♡ three hearts
3♢ three diamonds
3♣ three clubs
2NT two No Trumps
2♠ two spades
2♡ two hearts
2♢ two diamonds
2♣ two clubs
1NT one No Trump
1♠ one spade
1♡ one heart
1♢ one diamond
1♣ one club

The bidding can never go beyond seven because there are only thirteen tricks to play for and your contract is always for six tricks plus the number you bid.

HAND EVALUATION

To **open** the **bidding**, i.e. to be the first player to make a positive bid rather than just pass, you should have a little bit better than an average hand. An average hand would include one ace, one king, one queen etc.

The smaller cards are relatively unimportant but you need a way to compare the value of, say, two kings against one ace, or two queens against a king and a jack. As a guide to this you can use something called the **point count**. The high cards are each given a value, as follows (**1**):

Ace = 4
King = 3
Queen = 2
Jack = 1

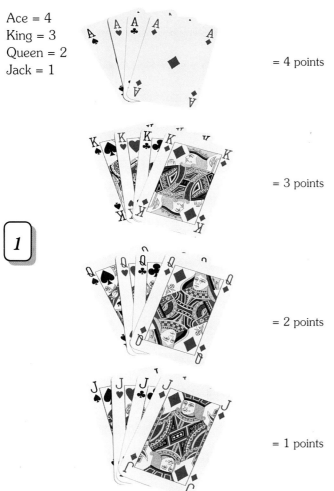

= 4 points

= 3 points

1

= 2 points

= 1 points

This gives a good idea of the relative value of the cards. An ace is worth roughly two queens; an ace plus a queen is roughly the equivalent of two kings.

You will see that there are ten points, or to be more precise **high card points** (HCP), in each suit, so forty in the whole pack. To open the bidding you should have at least a good twelve points, or compensating distribution. You will remember that long cards in a suit can produce extra tricks. You can allow for this by adding one point for each card in excess of four in a suit when you are considering your opening bid (i.e. one extra point for a five-card suit, two for a six-card suit etc). So (**2**) is 15 points.

2

While (**3**) is 18 points.

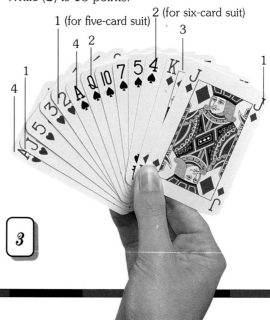

3

At this stage, a short suit is worth nothing; it may after all be opposite partner's long suit in which case it could even prove to be a liability, making it less likely that you have a good trump fit. However, suppose that partner bids a suit that you also like. Now a shortage in another suit could be useful as you can hope to make extra tricks by ruffing partner's losers in that suit.

When you have ample trumps and are supporting partner you can add points for shortages in other suits.

Doubleton (two cards) = 1 point
Singleton (one card) = 3 points
Void (no cards) = 5 points

Shortage points should be counted *instead* of, not as well as, length points.

So if partner opens 1♡,

hand (**4**) is worth 13 points (add one for the doubleton club suit) and hand (**5**) is worth 16 points (add three for the singleton club) in support of hearts.

Hand (**6**) is worth only 11 points in support of hearts as you do not have adequate trump support. You could, however, count extra length points for the spades and diamonds and treat your hand as being worth 13 points, just as if you were opening the bidding, as long as you intend to keep bidding your own suits.

The point count is also a useful guide to help you to decide how high to bid. Should you try for game or slam or settle for a quiet partscore? These are the total point counts required (HCP plus length or shortage points) between the two hands to make game or slam a fair bet. With less than the points for game, settle for a partscore.

3NT: 25 points
4♡/♠: 26 points
5♣/♢: 28 points
Any small slam: 33 points
Grand slam: 37+ points

OPENING THE BIDDING

To open the bidding, i.e. be the first player to make a positive call rather than just pass, you need to have a slightly better than average hand. If balanced, that means about twelve or more HCP, though a poor twelve should probably be passed.

The point count can be shaded slightly with a distributional hand. Holding a reasonable six-card suit or two five-card suits, you can afford to open all eleven point hands and, where the high cards are in your long suits, some hands with only ten points. Eleven points and one five-card suit, is the border line. With 5-3-3-2 shape pass, while 5-4-3-1 is usually worth a bid but 5-4-2-2 only if the high cards are in your long suits. As you gain experience you will discover that high cards in your long suits tend to be more valuable in the play than if they are in your shorter suits.

So, having decided to open the bidding, what bid should you choose?

A balanced hand, 4-3-3-3, 4-4-3-2, or 5-3-3-2 with 15-17 HCP should open 1NT, showing the all-round nature of the hand. All other hands of up to about 20 total points should be opened with one of your longest suit. Even stronger hands will be dealt with later.

Suppose you have two or more suits of equal length. With two five-card suits you are very keen that one of them should become the trump suit. You plan to show both and get your partner to choose between them. Unless you are very lucky, partner's first response will be in one of your short suits. Look at these sequences:

You	Partner	You	Partner
1♠	2♣	1♡	2♣
2♡		2♠	

The first is more economical because partner can choose either suit at the two level, either by passing or by bidding 2♠. In the second sequence, he would have to bid 3♡ if that was his preferred suit, pushing the bidding higher.

So the rule is to open the higher of two five-card suits, making a more convenient second bid. The one exception is that with spades and clubs you should open 1♣. Again 1♣ – 1◇/♡ – 1♠ is more economical than 1♠ –2◇/♡ – 3♣.

Holding two four-card suits, you have a balanced hand so are less certain that one of your suits must be trumps. Your plan should be to bid one suit, then bid No Trumps next time to show your all-round hand if no fit has yet been found. Best is to open the lower of two four-card suits. Partner may, for example, find it easy to respond 1♠ to a 1♡ opening but less easy to respond 2♡ to a 1♠ opening, so with four-four in hearts and spades 1♡ is the opening which best caters to finding a fit in either suit.

With three four-card suits, open the middle one with a black singleton and 1♣ with a red singleton. This is the best way to cater for all possible trump suits as you will always have a convenient rebid if partner responds in your short suit.

QUIZ ON OPENING BIDS

What would you open with the following (**1-10**)?

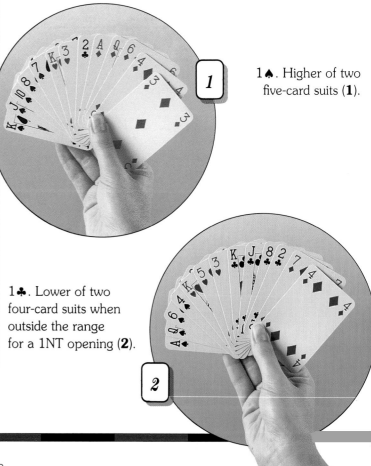

1

1♠. Higher of two five-card suits (**1**).

1♣. Lower of two four-card suits when outside the range for a 1NT opening (**2**).

2

1NT. This shows a balanced 15-17 HCP (**3**).

1♡. Middle of three touching suits (**7**).

1♣. The exception; with 5-5 in the black suits, open 1♣ (**4**).

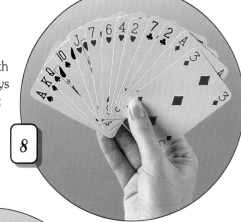

1♡. Remember, length before strength. Always open your longest suit even if another looks stronger (**8**).

Pass. There are no useful intermediates (tens and nines) and all the strength is in the short suits. Best to pass a bad twelve points (**5**).

Pass. 5-5 with 10 HCP can be opened but not with most of the strength in the short suits (**9**).

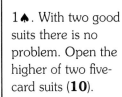

1◊. With strength in the long suits plus useful intermediates, open a flat twelve point hand with the lower of two four-card suits (**6**).

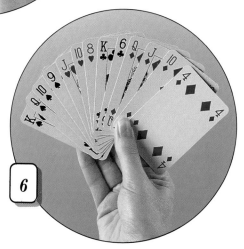

1♠. With two good suits there is no problem. Open the higher of two five-card suits (**10**).

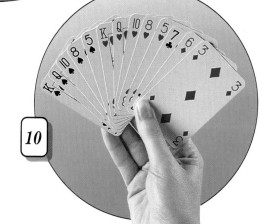

ONE OF A SUIT – THE FIRST RESPONSE

To make a game contract a good bet, your partnership needs roughly the following combined strength:

    3NT :   25+ points
    4♡/♠ :   26+ points
    5♣/♢ :   28+ points

These are total points including distributional points. In the case of the trump contracts, you also need an adequate trump fit, usually at least eight cards between the two hands.

When partner opens one of a suit he or she can have a very wide range of hand types, both in terms of high card strength and distribution. As he may have as many as 19 or 20 points and 25 or 26 is sufficient for game, you need to respond whenever you have six or more – just to give him another chance. If you have 0-5 points, you normally just pass as game is unlikely and any bid you make will make him think you are stronger than you are.

RESPONDING WITH WEAK HANDS (6-9 POINTS)

With a hand of this strength, you have three choices. You can:
- Raise partner's suit to the two level
- Bid 1NT
- Bid a new suit at the one level.

You cannot bid a new suit at the two level as you would be raising the level of the bidding with no guarantee of finding a fit. To do this you should have extra strength, normally a good 10+ points.

If partner opens with one of a major, you should always raise with four-card support even if you have a longer suit of your own. Remember that partner must also hold at least four cards in his suit so between you you will have at least eight.

Your second choice should be to bid a new suit at the one level in the hope that partner can support you. To do this you must hold at least four cards in

the suit. This is an absolute rule; the first person to bid a suit should always have at least four cards in it.

If partner opens one of a minor, bid a four-card or longer major even if you have support for his minor. Major suit contracts score better than minors and you can always support his suit later.

If you cannot support partner or bid a new suit at the one level, respond 1NT.

There is an important difference between a bid in partner's suit or No Trumps and a bid in a new suit. When you bid No Trumps or support partner you can make what is called a **limit bid**, showing both your shape and strength in one go. 1♡ – 2♡ and 1♡ – 1NT both show precisely 6-9 points and partner need not bid again if he does not wish to, i.e. your bid is **non-forcing**. A bid in a new suit, however, is completely unlimited. You may have only 6-9 points, but may equally well have a stronger hand and are going slowly to explore for a trump fit. A new suit response cannot be passed; it is **forcing** on partner to bid again.

QUIZ ON RESPONSES

What would you respond to 1♡ on hands (**1-5**)?

2♡. This shows heart support and 6-9 points (**1**).

2♡. This is the exception to the rule that support promises four cards. You are too weak to bid 2♣ and 2♡ looks to be easier to make than 1NT because of your singleton spade (**2**).

Did you say 2♡? That shows precisely 6-9 points and partner can pass it. As we will see shortly, with 10+ points you have to bid more strongly. In this case, though you could not have known, 3♡ (**5**).

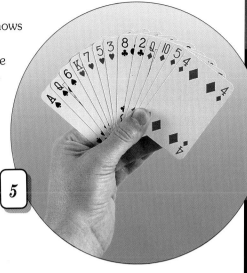

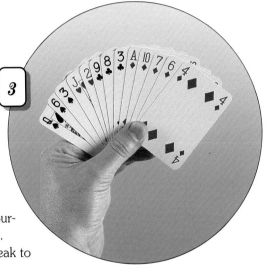

1NT. 6-9 points, fairly balanced and denying either heart support or a four-card spade suit. You are too weak to bid 2♢ (**3**).

If partner opens 1♢, how would you respond on these hands (**6-7**)?

1♡. You can support diamonds later; remember that partner must bid over a new suit response. First, look for a heart fit (**6**).

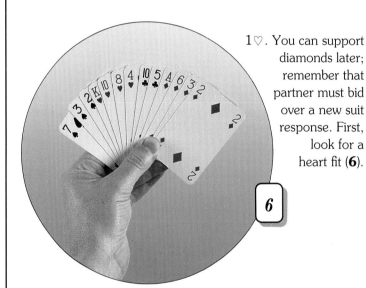

1♠. Always bid a four-card suit at the one level in preference to 1NT. Remember partner must bid again over 1♠ (**4**).

1♠. Spades are not your longest suit, but you are not strong enough to bid the clubs; that shows 10+ points (**7**).

ONE OF A SUIT – RESPONDING WITH STRONGER HANDS

With 10+ points you obviously have a stronger hand, and in responding to an opening bid of one of a suit, you have the following options:

(i) Jump in partner's suit. A raise to the three level shows 10-12 points and is **invitational**. In other words, partner passes with a minimum opening hand and goes to game with something to spare. A raise to the four level shows 13-15 points and, if it is in a major, is a game bid so partner normally passes. If it is in a minor, it is highly invitational.

(ii) Jump in No Trumps. A jump to 2NT shows 10-12 HCP and is invitational. It shows a balanced hand with less than four cards in partner's suit or any unbid major which you could have bid at the one level. A jump to 3NT shows 13-15 HCP and, as it is a game bid, partner is allowed to pass. Again, you are balanced and do not have support for partner.

(iii) Bid a new suit at the one level. As before this shows at least four cards and 6+ points. It forces partner to bid again.

(iv) Bid a new suit at the two level. This shows 10+ points, is your longest suit, and forces partner to bid again.

Note that a new suit at the one level shows 6+ points, not 6-9. It is not necessary to bid at the two level just to show 10+ points. So in response to 1♢, bid 1♡ with this hand (**1**) not 2♡. The jump in a new suit has a special meaning which we will look at later.

If you think you have a close choice between two or more responses:

• Always support partner's major if you can do so.
• Second choice is to bid a new major suit.
• Third choice is to support partner's minor.
• If none of the above is possible, make a limit bid in No Trumps if balanced. Don't bother to bid a new minor if you have only four in a balanced hand.

• When raising partner or bidding No Trumps, *always bid the full value of your hand immediately.* 1♡ – 3♡/2NT shows 10-12 points precisely; if you bid it with 14, partner passes and you miss a game, it is your fault. Limit bids are very useful, but only if used correctly.

QUIZ ON RESPONSES

Partner opens 1♡ – what do you bid on these hands (**2-6**)?

3♡. Though you are completely balanced you must support partner's major. 3♡ shows 10-12 points and is invitational (**2**).

Pass. You have four-card support but only four points – not enough to bid (**3**).

2NT. Do not bother with a four-card minor when you are so balanced and have strength in all the unbid suits. 2NT shows 10-12 balanced (**6**).

4♡. Only 11 HCP, but 14 points in all once you allow for the singleton, so you know there are 26+ between you – enough for game (**4**).

Partner opens 1◇ – what do you bid with these hands (**7-8**)?

2♣. Yes, majors are more important than minors, but where possible you should always bid your longest suit first. You can always bid the spades next time (**7**).

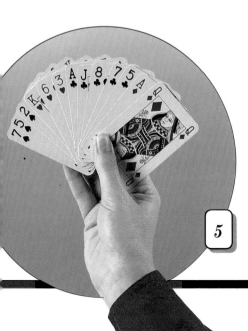

2♣. A five-card minor is always worth showing when you cannot support partner (**5**).

3NT. True, you have four-card diamond support, but 5◇ is a lot harder to make than 3NT. You are completely balanced so try for the nine trick game. Partner can always bid again if he is very unbalanced (**8**).

OPENER'S REBID OPPOSITE A LIMIT BID

The next stage we must look at is what to do as opener when your partner has raised you in your bid suit. You obviously both like the same trump suit, so the only question is whether to settle for a safe partscore or try for game. Responder is known to have only 6-9 points so opener adds his points to this to see if there are the required 26+ between the two hands.

RESPONDER RAISED OPENER'S SUIT – 1♡ – 2♡ (6-9)

How should opener rebid over a limit bid from partner?

(i) With less than 16 opener passes, e.g.

- ♠ AQ5
- ♡ AK732
- ◇ 952
- ♣ 64

(ii) With 19+ she bids game, e.g.

- ♠ AQJ5
- ♡ AK732
- ◇ A8
- ♣ J2

(iii) With 16-18 she does not know if game is on or not. It will be opposite 8-9, but not opposite 6-7. Opener invites game by bidding 1♡ – 2♡ – 3♡ and responder should pass with a minimum but bid 4♡ with a maximum, e.g. bid 3♡ on:

- ♠ A98
- ♡ AQJ64
- ◇ KQ3
- ♣ J8

After 1♡ – 2♡ – 3♡, responder bids 4♡ with (A) but passes with (B) in this example (1).

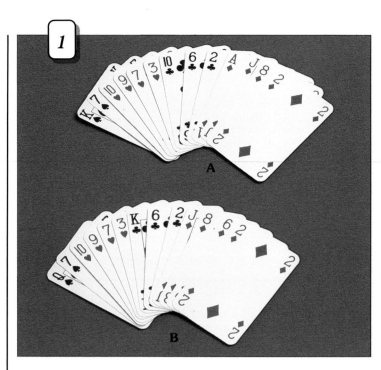

RESPONDER RAISED OPENER'S SUIT – 1♡ – 3♡ (10-12)

3♡ shows 10-12 points so is much more encouraging than 2♡. With a minimum opening bid, opener passes; with extra values she bids 4♡. A reasonable guide is for opener mentally to take a king away from her hand, turning it into a small card. If this still leaves an opening bid, she has enough to spare to go on to game, otherwise she passes. So, bid 4♡ with (2) but pass with (3).

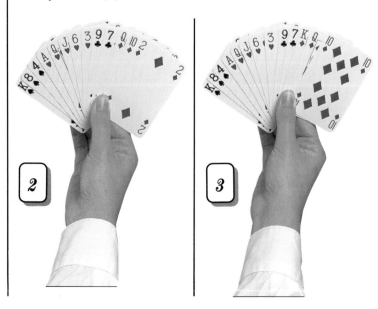

RESPONDER RAISED OPENER'S SUIT –
1♡ – 4♡ (13-15)

As 4♡ is game, there is no point bidding higher unless there is a slam on, requiring at least twelve tricks and therefore at most one loser. Unless she is very strong, opener will usually pass.

RESPONDER BID 1NT (6-9)

1NT shows 6-9 points and a fairly balanced hand. If also fairly balanced, opener simply adds the points together. With 12-16 she passes as there are unlikely to be the 25 required for game. With 17-18, she cannot be sure about game. She raises to 2NT to invite game, expecting responder to pass with 6-7 points but bid 3NT with 8-9. So after 1♡ – 1NT – 2NT. responder bids 3NT with (**4**) but passes with (**5**):

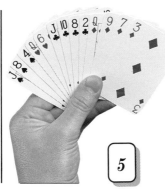

Holding 19+ points, opener raises a 1NT response to 3NT.

If opener is unbalanced she will not wish to play in No Trumps. She may rebid a six-card suit or bid a second suit of four cards or more to give partner a choice. With a strong hand, 17+, opener can jump to show her extra strength. After 1♡ – 1NT – here are some examples of how you should rebid (**6-9**).

(**6**) Bid 2♡, which partner should pass.

(**7**) Bid 3♡ to show six hearts and invite game.

(**8**) Bid 2◇, giving partner a choice. Remember that this must show five hearts, else you would pass 1NT.

(**9**) Bid 3◇, showing a strong distributional hand.

RESPONDER BID 2NT (10-12)

The response is invitational and balanced. Opener passes with a minimum balanced hand and raises to 3NT with a good 14+. A simple rebid of her original suit is to play, showing at least six but a minimum hand, while any new suit bid or jump is forcing.

RESPONDER BID 3NT (13-15)

3NT is game so unless opener is very strong and envisages a slam, she can just pass. However, an unbalanced hand should not play in No Trumps (**10, 11**).

(**10**) Should bid 4♡ – partner must have at least two.

(**11**) Should bid 4◇, asking partner to bid 4♡ or 5◇. He cannot pass 4◇ as there must be the strength for game between the two hands.

OPENER'S REBID OPPOSITE A NEW SUIT RESPONSE AT THE ONE LEVEL

When partner's response is in a new suit, opener must bid again. Though responder may only have a bare six points, he is completely unlimited and may have a very strong hand with which he needs a second, and perhaps third chance to bid to describe it fully.

Opener's rebid should give extra information about her shape and strength. In other words, if she has opened 1♡ to say "I have 12-20 points and at least four hearts", to rebid 2♡ to say "I have 12-20 points and at least four hearts", is silly; you must tell partner something new.

Your first choice should always be to support partner's suit if you have four of them and, occasionally, even with only three. As always, when you support partner you make a limit bid, showing your strength as well as your shape. After 1◇ – 1♠ –?

2♠ = 12-15 total points
3♠ = 16-18 total points
4♠ = 19+ total points

Responder may pass any of these limit bids but will go on to game if he can see that the combined point count is sufficient.

Jump raises should always promise four-card trump support, but a simple raise, 1◇ – 1♠ – 2♠, may occasionally be made with only three, e.g. (**1**).

With a fairly balanced hand with less than four cards in partner's suit, rebid in No Trumps. Again, you make a limit bid, showing your strength.

1◇ – 1♠ – 1NT = 12-14
– 2NT = 17-18
– 3NT = 19-20

(Remember that with 15-17 points and a balanced hand, you would have *opened* 1NT not 1◇.) Now look at examples **2** and **3**.

(**2**) is flat with no intermediates and should open 1NT. (**3**) has a five-card suit and good intermediates so is worth 1◇ followed by 2NT.

You may decide to rebid your original suit. By bidding it again you guarantee extra length in it, always at least five cards and usually six. Where possible you should give partner a choice by bidding a second suit rather than repeat your first suit. Remember that he knows you will have opened your longest suit so will know to go back to it if he has equal length in your two suits. A simple rebid of your first suit shows 12-15 points and a long suit in an unbalanced hand.

(i)   ♠   J8   (ii)   ♠   J8
      ♡   A63   ♡   K63
      ♢   AQ1074   ♢   AQ10742
      ♣   KJ2   ♣   K2

Hand (i) has a fifth diamond but is essentially a balanced hand and a 1NT opening is more descriptive than 1♢ then 2♢. Hand (ii), however, has a sixth diamond and now 1♢ then 2♢ is the best sequence of bids.

With 16-18 points and a reasonable six-card suit you can jump in your suit, 1♢ – 1♠ – 3♢. This bid is not forcing but is highly invitational. A typical example would be (**4**).

With a second suit, you should bid it whenever possible to give partner a choice. Say you hold hand (**5**)

1♢ – 1♠ – 2♢ tells partner only that you are minimum with five diamonds. 1♢ – 1♠ – 2♣ not only shows four clubs but virtually guarantees the fifth diamond. With 4-4 you would usually be balanced and bidding No Trumps. Clearly, 2♣ gives much more information than 2♢.

You have to differentiate between rebids which raise the level of the auction beyond the next level of your first suit and those which do not. After 1♢ – 1♠ – 2♣, partner can choose either of your suits at the two level, either by passing or by bidding 2♢. After 1♢ – 1♠ – 2♡, he would need to go to the three level if he preferred your first suit.

Rebids which push the bidding up need to be stronger as you will need to make more tricks. The rule is that a rebid above two of your first suit shows 16+ HCP and is strong, while a rebid below two of your first suit need not have extra values.

1♢ – 1♠ – 2♣ may be minimum
1♢ – 1♠ – 2♡ shows a strong hand
1♢ – 1♠ – 3♣ shows a strong hand

After 1♢ – 1♠ , hand (**6A**) can comfortably bid 2♡, showing five diamonds and four hearts with extra strength. Hand (**6B**) must rebid 2♢. It is not strong enough to risk pushing the bidding higher by bidding 2♡.

This is one of the trickiest concepts in bidding, so do not worry if it seems strange at first. Just remember that the higher you bid, the more tricks you will have to make. It makes sense that whoever pushes the bidding higher needs to have the extra strength to make those tricks.

4

5

6A

6B

OPENER'S REBID AFTER A NEW SUIT RESPONSE AT THE TWO LEVEL

Again, because the response was in a new suit, opener must bid again. Because he has taken the bidding up a level, responder has promised more strength than when he bids at the one level. This time he has shown 10+ points so you do not need very much extra for game to be a real possibility.

As always, you usually support your partner's suit if you can do so and, of course, you must show the strength of your hand at the same time. 1♡ – 2♣ – ?

3♣ = 12-15 total points
4♣ = 16-18 total points
5♣ = 19+ total points

Responder may pass any of these limit bids but will go on to game if he thinks the combined strength is present.

A balanced hand rebids in No Trumps. 1♡ – 2♣ – ?

2NT = 12-14 HCP
3NT = 17-19 HCP

Do not worry if you are weak in an unbid suit; it is still best to describe the all-round nature of your hand to partner, i.e. rebid 2NT with hand (**1**).

When partner's response is in a minor it can occasionally be correct to rebid in No Trumps despite having support for his suit. It is fine to bid 1♡ – 2♣ – 4♣

on hand (**2**) where you have a distributional hand and 3NT looks unlikely. Five of a minor is often hard to make, however, as you can only afford two losers, while 3NT may be easier if you have every suit covered. Hand (**3**) should rebid 2NT, showing a balanced 12-14, rather than 3♣. If partner is very distributional he will bid another suit so you can still get to 5♣ when it is correct.

You can rebid your original suit to show extra length. 1♡ – 2♣ – 2♡ shows at least five hearts and 12-15 total points. Partner need not bid again if he is also minimum.

A jump rebid shows a six-card suit and is highly invitational, about 16-17 total points. Partner should only pass if he is both minimum and dislikes hearts. A typical hand for 1♡ – 2♣ – 3♡ might be (**4**). Alternatively you may bid a second suit. The rules for doing this are much the same as when partner's response was at the one level. If you have a second four-card suit you should normally bid it rather than repeat your first suit as you give partner more information. You must be careful not to go beyond two of your first suit unless you have extra values.

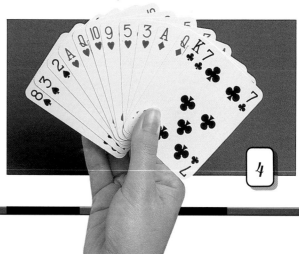

QUIZ ON REBIDS

After 1♡ – 2♣ – ? what should you bid on the following hands (**5-8**)?

No problem, bid 2♠ to show your shape and extra strength (**5**).

Rebid 2♡ (**6**). You need about 16 total points to bid 2♠ because it pushes the bidding higher. Indeed, after a two over one response this **reverse** bid, as it is known, is usually treated as forcing on the partnership to reach game. After all, you know opener has 16+ points and responder 10+, so with 26+ between you, why not?

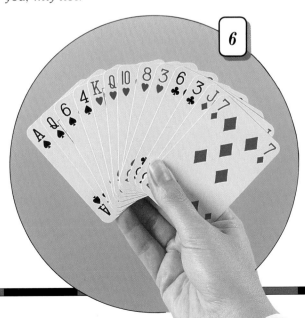

3◇. 2◇ would show 12-15 and be non-forcing. The jump in a new suit shows 16+ and forces partner to keep bidding (**7**).

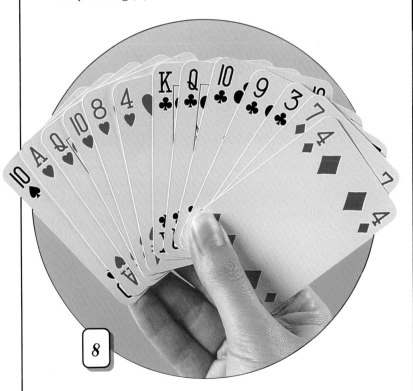

2♡. 3♣ would raise the level of the bidding and, like all bids above 2♡, shows extra values. All you can do is rebid your first suit (**8**).

RESPONDER'S REBID

By the time it comes to responder's second bid, he has heard two bids from his partner so has a lot of information about her shape and strength. Often, responder is in a position to choose the final contract immediately. If he is not, he may bid a new suit or make an invitational bid in No Trumps or one of partner's suits to invite her opinion.

There are too many possible sequences to look at every one in detail so let's try to get a feel for the general approach responder should adopt.

IF GAME IS OUT OF REACH

Where opener's rebid clearly shows that the partnership cannot have enough combined strength for game, responder should pick the safest looking partscore at the lowest possible level. Examine hands (**1-5**) and decide what you might rebid.

After 1♡ – 1♠ – 2♢, bid 2♡. True, your diamonds are stronger than your hearts, but partner is sure to have five hearts – her first suit – but may only have four diamonds (**1**).

After 1♡ – 1♠ – 2♠, Pass. Partner has shown four-card spade support but a minimum hand so there can be no game (**2**).

After 1♢ – 1♠ – 1NT, Pass. 2♠ could be better but you have no way of knowing if partner has three spades or only two (**3**).

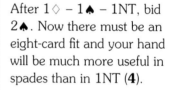

After 1♢ – 1♠ – 1NT, bid 2♠. Now there must be an eight-card fit and your hand will be much more useful in spades than in 1NT (**4**).

After 1♢ – 1♠ – 1NT, bid 2♡. This is a weak bid which asks partner to pass or bid 2♠ according to which suit she prefers. You must have an eight-card fit in one of your suits. (**5**).

RESPONDER IS UNSURE ABOUT GAME

Where responder thinks there may be enough combined strength for game but then again there may not, he makes an invitational bid. Normally, opener will pass this with a minimum but bid game with a maximum. Look at examples (**6-9**).

After 1♡ – 1♠ – 2♢, bid 3♡. This shows about 10-12 points, just like an immediate 1♡ – 3♡ bid, but only three-card support. Don't worry, partner has promised five hearts by rebidding in a new suit (**6**).

After 1♡ – 1♠ – 1NT, raise to 2NT. She will know this is invitational because you would just pass 1NT with no game interest (**7**).

After 1♠ – 2♣ – 2♡, bid 3♡, showing four hearts and about 10-12 points (**8**).

After 1♡ – 1♠ – 2♡, bid 3♡ to invite game. Partner has at least five hearts and probably six for her rebid (**9**).

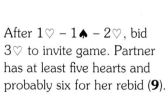

RESPONDER IS SURE OF GAME

When responder knows the partnership has game values, he must either bid game or bid a new suit to force partner to bid again. Remember, any bid in No Trumps or in one of partner's suits is a limit bid which partner can pass. Do not take that risk if you know you should be in game (**10-12**).

After 1♡ – 1♠ – 2♣, jump to 3NT. There does not look to be a good trump fit, but between you, you have all four suits well covered (**10**).

After 1♢ – 1♠ – 1NT jump to 3♡. A simple 2♡ would not be forcing. Facing 12-14, you want to reach game but need partner to choose between your suits. Jump to force her to bid (**11**).

After 1♡ – 2♣ – 2♡, bid 2♠. No Trumps will only be good if she can bid it – look at your diamonds. Meanwhile, what is to stop her having four cards in spades (**12**)?

HAND EVALUATION

So far we have talked about counting points. We have already seen that there is more to life than holding high cards. When you have a fit for partner's suit, a shortage in another suit can be useful as it allows you to trump his losers in that suit. When faced with a borderline decision, there are other factors you could take into consideration.

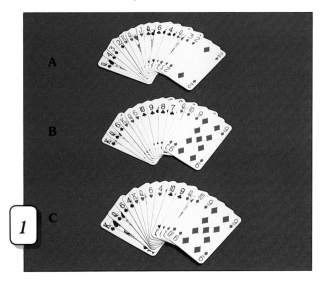

I would open hands (**1B**) and (**C**) but not (**A**). (**A**) is the worst possible shape, 4-3-3-3, giving only one possible trump suit and one possible suit to produce length tricks in No Trumps. It has no intermediates (10s, 9s, 8s) and a lot of unsupported honours. The problem with unsupported honours is that they need a lot of help from partner's hand before you can make many tricks in the suit. Put hand (**A**) opposite North's hand shown in (**2**) and try to make 3NT, despite the combined 25 HCP. In every suit except hearts you can set up one trick easily but setting up more than one will probably also mean establishing extra tricks for the defence.

Hand (**B**) is better because there are nice intermediates plus all the honours are in combination, backed up by other honours. If partner has as little as the jack of either major, you have a suit you can attack and establish extra tricks for your side without doing the same for your opponents.

Hand (**C**) is even better because now your honour combinations are in longer suits so you have a better

chance of tricks from length as well as strength if partner has a major suit jack or better. Also, in the bidding you have two chances of finding a trump fit instead of only one.

Look at hands (**3, 4, 5**). Each time you add a card to your long suit, you give yourself a more secure trump suit but also add a potential extra length trick. Hand (**5**) is likely to produce a trick more than hand (**4**) which in turn is a trick better than hand (**3**).

Hand (**7**) is much more powerful than (**6**). Having strength in your long suits makes it very easy to establish the extra length tricks in those suits, as in (**7**) where you hope to make the ♠32 and ♡8 as well as the high cards. In (**6**) the high cards are only producing strength tricks. Look at how much work will be required to establish the little spades or hearts.

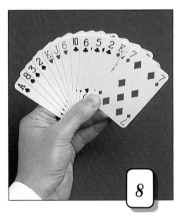

Now look at these examples (**8, 9**). The bidding goes:

$$1♡ \; — 1♠$$
$$2♢ \; — ?$$

Your shape and high card strength is identical yet your choice of bid should be quite different.

You know there is an eight-card heart fit and near game values. Hand (**9**) has high cards in partner's suits plus an ace opposite one of her short suits.

Although you are a point light, you might upgrade this beautifully fitting hand and jump to 4♡. Opposite a complete minimum such as:

♠　94
♡　AQ975
♢　AQ83
♣　73

4♡ is excellent. You hope to make five hearts, three diamonds, one spade and a diamond ruff – ten in all.

Put the same opening hand opposite hand (**9**). Now (**10**), 4♡ would need both red finesses plus a 3-2 heart break – heavily against the odds. This time you have no high cards in partner's suits so your points are much less useful. Despite the known eight-card heart fit, you should probably bid 2NT over 2♢. In No Trumps your high cards will all be useful while in a heart contract they may not.

The message here is that if partner's suit is to be trumps, then high cards in his suits can be more useful than elsewhere.

So with a borderline decision always look not only at how many points you have but also at where they are.

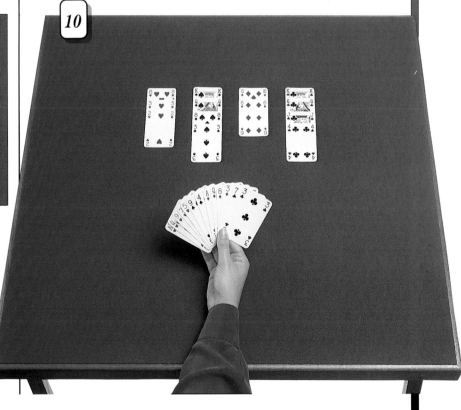

THE 1NT OPENING BID

The 1NT opening is a special opening bid in that it is effectively a limit bid. In other words, it describes both the shape and strength of the hand within quite narrow limits immediately. It promises 15-17 points (some prefer to agree 16-18 but the difference is a minor one – as long as you agree beforehand) and a balanced hand.

The definition of a balanced hand is 4-3-3-3, 4-4-3-2 or 5-3-3-2 shape. It does not matter if you have a suit with no high card in it, but if you have a five-card suit it should not be a very strong one, e.g. Q7532 is acceptable but AQJ108 is not – with a strong five-card suit prefer to bid and rebid it. Have a look at these examples (**1-5**).

(**3**) Open 1NT despite the fact that all your strength is in two suits. 1NT tells partner your strength and general handtype immediately.

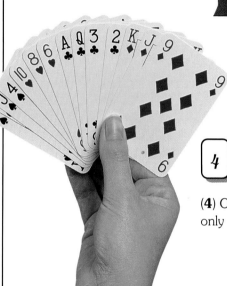

(**4**) Open 1♣ as you have only 14 HCP.

(**1**) Open 1NT despite the five-card heart suit, as most of the strength is elsewhere.

(**2**) With such strong hearts it is best to open 1♡.

(**5**) A borderline hand because of the good suit, but with stoppers in all four suits you should treat this as a balanced hand and the useful five-card suit makes it worth fifteen points and a 1NT opening.

Because 1NT is such a precise opening, unlike one of a suit, a special scheme of responses is needed. Actually, this is largely much simpler than after a one of a suit opening.

RESPONDING WITH BALANCED HANDS

With a balanced hand, responder can simply add his points to the 15-17 promised by opener and decide how high to go. With 0-7 points he passes as there cannot be the minimum 25 points required for game between the two hands.

With 8-9 points responder raises to 2NT. This invites game. Opener is expected to pass with a minimum opening but go on to game with a maximum.

With 10-15 points responder raises to 3NT which opener must pass. There must be at least 25 points between the two hands but cannot be sufficient for a slam.

With 16-17 points, raise to 4NT. There may or may not be enough for slam so responder makes an invitational bid. Opener is expected to pass with a minimum opening but bid 6NT with a maximum.

Finally, with 18+ points, responder can jump straight to slam.

RESPONDER IS UNBALANCED

If responder has a long suit (5+ cards) he can be sure that he is facing some support so it may well be better to have that suit as trumps rather than play in No Trumps.

With a weak hand, responder can bid his long suit, 2◇, 2♡ or 2♠, and opener must pass. You are saying that you think two of your suit will be a better bet than 1NT and are not asking partner's opinion. Contrary to normal procedure, the weaker you are the more case there is for bidding. Say you hold (**6**). How many tricks do you think your hand will be worth in 1NT? And how many in 2♡?

Hopefully, you can see that it may make three or four tricks eventually in 2♡ but be completely useless in 1NT. With 0-7 points, a "weak takeout" of two of a suit is fine. With a stronger hand you should think of game. With a five-card minor suit in a fairly balanced hand, raise to the appropriate level of No Trumps. Five of a minor is a very long way to go, so it is better to try for 3NT. Four of a major is a much more realistic alternative to 3NT, so when you have a five-card major you want to suggest the idea to partner. Two of a suit is weak, as we have seen. Not to worry, jump to three of any suit and it shows a game-going hand with at least a fair five-card suit and asks partner to choose between 3NT and game in your suit. She is forced to bid. If you hold say, ♠AJ1064, ♡K63, ◇J52, ♣103, bid 3♠ and expect partner to raise with three or more card support, or otherwise go back to 3NT.

THE STAYMAN CONVENTION

You may have noticed that we said that 1NT – 2◇/♡/♠ were weak bids based on a long suit. There was no mention of 1NT – 2♣. This is because 2♣ is a special bid. It is called Stayman after the man who first publicized the idea, Samuel Stayman, though it was actually his partner George Rapee, who invented it.

So far we have seen how the responder to 1NT bids with a balanced hand and when he has a long suit to bid. The trouble is that, as we have seen, playing in a 4-4 trump fit can be extremely effective, yet this scheme does not cater for reaching such a fit. Rapee and Stayman realized that it was the major suit fits which really mattered; usually, if you have only a 4-4 fit in a minor or if you can make five of the minor, you can also make 3NT. The idea of Stayman is very simple; a 2♣ response to a 1NT opening asks partner if she holds four cards in a major suit. The responses are:

2◇ – No four-card major
2♡ – Four cards in hearts, says nothing about spades
2♠ – Four cards in spades, denies four hearts

The only cost of this artificial bid is that you cannot make a weakness takeout into 2♣. Instead you bid 2♣, which partner will take as Stayman, then bid 3♣ over her response. This cancels the first message and says you wanted to play in clubs all along. Because you are going to the three level when partner might only hold a doubleton, you really need six clubs to bid this way.

CONTINUATIONS AFTER STAYMAN

Unless you have the weak hand with a long club suit, you should always be strong enough at least to invite game if you use Stayman, i.e. at least eight points. You should also hold at least one four-card major, else why bother with Stayman? When you hear partner's reply you can either bid game directly or invite it.

Say you hold hand (**1**). You respond 2♣ (Stayman) to partner's 1NT opening. If he bids 2◇ you know there is no fit, so bid 3NT; if he bids 2♡ or 2♠ you raise to four of that suit. In all cases, partner must pass.

Now take away the king of diamonds, leaving (**2**). Now you bid 2NT over 2◇, invitational just as though you had raised 1NT to 2NT directly; and raise 2♡ or 2♠ to three of the suit, also invitational. In each case partner goes on to game with a maximum but passes with a minimum.

QUIZ ON STAYMAN

In each auction, what is your next bid with this hand (**3**)?

(A)	1NT—2♣ ?	(C)	1NT—2♣ 2♡—3♡ ?
(B)	1NT—2♣ 2♡—2NT ?	(D)	1NT—3♠ ?

(A) 2♡. 2♣ was Stayman so you must bid your four-card major.

(B) Pass. Partner has used Stayman and you have shown your heart suit. Now 2NT says partner does not have four hearts, or else he would have supported them, but is of invitational strength. As you are minimum (15 HCP) you pass.

(C) Pass. Again partner is inviting game, though this time he does have heart support. You are still minimum so must again pass.

(D) 4♠. You do not need four cards to support partner when he bids his own suit because he has promised five. A jump in a suit by responder is forcing and as you know there is an eight-card fit you raise to 4♠.

In each auction, as responder what is your next bid with this hand (**4**)?

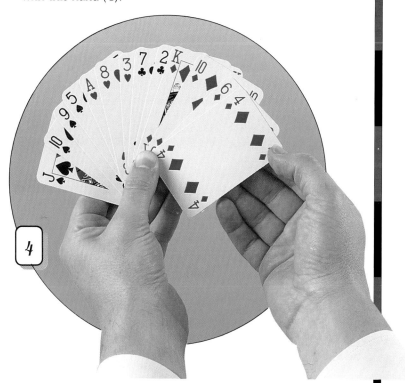

(E)	1NT—?	(G)	1NT—2♣ 2♡—?
(F)	1NT—2♣ 2◇—?	(H)	1NT—2♣ 2♠—?

(E) 2♣. You have enough strength to invite game and are balanced. You could raise to 2NT, but why not check for a 4-4 spade fit along the way?

(F) 2NT. Now that you know there is no spade fit, go back to Plan A, an invitational raise to 2NT.

(G) 2NT. Again, bid 2NT. Trust partner to work out that as you could not support hearts you must have spades. If she also has spades she will bid them – 3♠ with a minimum, 4♠ with a maximum.

(H) 3♠. Good news; you have found a spade fit. You are still only worth an invitational bid, however.

DEFENCE – THE OPENING LEAD

The opening lead is the most important single card played in most bridge hands, often deciding the eventual success or failure of the contract. It is also the most difficult card to choose. After the opening lead has been made, the dummy goes down and gives the other three players extra information on which to base their later decisions. The opening leader has only his own thirteen cards plus what clues may be gleaned from the bidding to guide him.

There are two parts to choosing an opening lead: which suit to lead and which card within that suit. We will look at the choice of suit later. That is very much a matter of judgement. For the moment, let us assume we have decided on the suit and concentrate on deciding which card to lead.

There are three basic types of suit you might hold. These are:

- A suit headed by two or more touching honour cards, e.g. QJ4 or KQJ2.
- A suit headed by at least one honour card but not in sequence (not touching), e.g. K743 or Q1065.
- A suit consisting entirely of small cards, e.g. 85 or 7643.

A suit headed by an honour sequence is a very attractive one as it has a good chance of establishing some tricks for your side while only rarely giving declarer an extra trick which he could not manage for himself. It is important that you lead one of the honours. If you led the two from KQJ2, declarer might win cheaply with the ten. If you lead any honour, he is obliged to use the ace if he wishes to win the trick.

A lead from a suit headed by an honour but not by a sequence is more risky. When you find partner with some help in the suit you can hope to establish tricks but equally you may present declarer with a free trick. In case partner has nothing, it is best to lead a small card. Suppose the suit is like this (**1**).If you lead the king, declarer gets three tricks for no losers. If you lead small, you have a chance to win the third round of the suit with your king.

A lead from a collection of small cards is relatively safe in that it rarely gives declarer something he could not take for himself, but it is unlikely to achieve very much in that it needs partner to have a very good holding if you are to establish tricks in the suit. Nonetheless, a safe lead can often be quite effective.

Declarer has a big edge over the defenders. He can see the combined assets of his hand and dummy and plan accordingly. The defenders cannot see each other's hands. They need to exchange as much information as possible with the cards they play to make the defence easier. Suppose you held KQJ (**2**) and led the one nearest your thumb. Partner would know you held some honour sequence but not exactly what. Wouldn't it help if you always led the same card from the same holding?

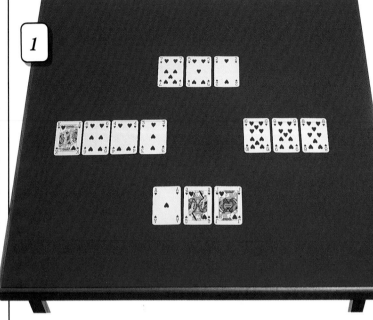

The normal agreement is always to lead the top of the sequence (**3**). So the king promises the queen but, in a suit contract, denies the ace; the queen promises the jack but denies the king; and so on.

When you do not have an honour sequence you lead a small card. From a suit headed by at least one honour (**4**) you lead a low one – for reasons we will see later, the agreement is to lead the fourth card from the top, e.g. 4 from KJ642 (**5**). From a suit consisting entirely of small cards (**6**) you lead the top one, top of nothing as it is known, e.g. 8 from 8764 (**7**). You also lead the top card from any doubleton. So if partner sees you lead a small spot card he knows you are interested in the suit and this will encourage him to lead it again later, while if he sees a high spot card he will know you are not interested so will look elsewhere.

RECOMMENDED TABLE OF LEADS

Suit holding	No trumps	Suit contract	Notes
AK4	K	A	In No Trumps, the
AKJ104	A	A	lead of an ace is a
			special lead, asking
			partner to drop an
			honour if he has one.
KQJ	K	K	Top of a sequence
QJ10	Q	Q	,,
J109	J	J	,,
1098	10	10	,,
KJ10	J	J	Top of an interior
			sequence
K109	10	10	,,
Q109	10	10	,,
K7	K	K	Top of a doubleton
K73	3	3	Small from an honour
K732	2	2	Fourth highest from an honour
K8732	3	3	,,
K108732	7	7	,,
108732	3	3	,,
A7532	3	A	Do not underlead an ace in a suit contract – you may not get a second chance if declarer is singleton.
73	7	7	Top of a doubleton
763	7	7	Top of nothing

3

4

5

6

7

OPENING LEADS IN NO TRUMPS

Your opponents play a No Trump contract. Which suit should you lead? You have two sources of information to help you to decide: your hand and the bidding. Firstly, the bidding.

- If your partner has bid a suit, you should usually lead it unless you have a very good alternative.
- If an opponent, particularly declarer, has bid a suit you should usually look elsewhere.
- An unbid suit is reasonably attractive as your opponents may have strength there but probably not any great length.

Secondly, your hand.

- The ideal is a long suit headed by a sequence of honours, establishing both high card and extra length tricks without giving declarer anything, e.g. KQJ94 or QJ1075.
- A sequence of honours in a short suit is safe but will produce a limited number of tricks. Nonetheless, KQJ or QJ10 is a better lead than a moderate four-card suit such as K764 or Q953.
- A long suit headed by one or more honours, e.g. KJ953, is a good lead. Even though the lead may sometimes give declarer a free trick, this will more than come back if you can eventually establish and cash your long cards.
- A suit consisting entirely of small cards needs a lot of help from partner if it is to produce any tricks. Still, with no long suit, no safe sequence, or perhaps where your long suit is one bid by an opponent, a passive lead from three or four small in an unbid suit may be best.

So look for a long suit where you might establish length tricks, just as though you were declarer. Remember you have a partner; what you want is to lead the suit where the partnership has the best combined holding, not necessarily just your own suit.

THE RULE OF ELEVEN

Knowing that partner will always lead fourth highest from a broken suit is useful. For example, if you see him lead a two, you know immediately that he cannot hold more than a four-card suit and can place declarer with the missing length. It is very valuable to be able to build up a picture of the two unseen hands in this way.

You can also use something called the **Rule of Eleven**. Suppose you decide that partner has led his fourth best card. You start with the "magic" number, eleven. Subtract the number of spots on the card partner leads. Next, count how many cards in your hand and dummy are higher than the one led. Subtract that number. The figure remaining is the number of cards in declarer's hand which are higher than the one led.

Sounds complicated? Let's look at an example (**1**).

Partner (West) leads the six and declarer plays dummy's three (**2**). Without the rule of eleven, you would be tempted to play the queen. Using it, however, you know to play the nine (**3**). Why?

(i) 11-6 (the card led) = 5
(ii) 5-2 (number of cards in dummy higher than the six) = 3
(iii) 3-3 (number of cards in your hand higher than the six) = 0

So declarer cannot have even one card higher than the six and your nine is guaranteed to win.

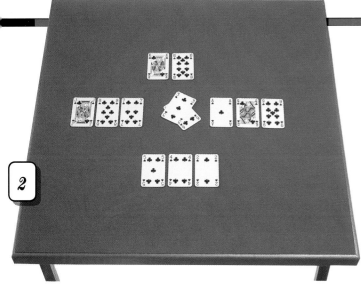

(**5**) ♠5. Again you have a good long suit to lead but this time no sequence. Lead your fourth highest.

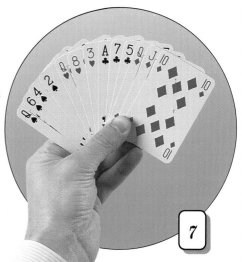

(**6**) ♠9. Dummy has bid your long heart suit, so there is unlikely to be much future there. With no other suit of your own, try to hit partner's suit with a Top of Nothing lead.

QUIZ ON OPENING LEADS

The bidding goes 1♡ – Pass – 1NT – All Pass. What should you lead holding these hands (**4-7**)?

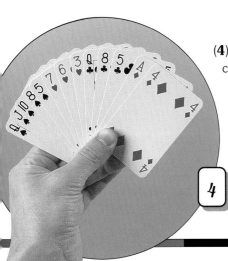

(**4**) ♠Q. When your length coincides with an honour sequence the choice of suit is an easy one. It is normal to lead the top of the sequence.

(**7**) ◇Q. Your long suit is only four cards and pretty weak. Rather than risk giving declarer a cheap trick in spades, lead a safe honour sequence.

OPENING LEADS IN SUIT CONTRACTS

Everything we have said already about opening leads applies also when leading against a suit contract but there are a few extra points to consider.

Against a No Trump contract you would be quite happy to lead low from a holding such as A7643. It is almost never right to do so in a suit contract. If the lead gives a trick away, that trick will be lost forever with no later compensation. Remember, in No Trumps you can hope to establish and eventually cash long tricks by exhausting everyone else of your long suit. In a suit contract they will simply ruff your established winner. So it would be reasonable to make a rule that you never underlead an ace as your opening lead in a suit contract. If you must lead the suit, cash the ace, but usually look elsewhere unless you also hold the king.

You should also be a little less willing to lead from a broken suit such as KJ864 or Q732 than you would be in No Trumps. While such an attacking lead will often be necessary, again there is the danger of giving declarer an extra trick for which you get no compensation so you need to use judgement as to when to take the risk.

There is also a new possibility, namely to lead a trump (**1, 2**). Consider that your opponents chose to play in a suit rather than No Trumps. They expected to profit from doing so, perhaps by having greater control thanks to the trump suit but also perhaps through making extra tricks by cross-trumping. If you can lead enough rounds of trumps you may be able to prevent declarer from making those extra tricks.

ACTIVE v PASSIVE LEADS

An active lead is an attacking lead, one which takes a risk but works well when partner has a suitable holding in the suit led. For example, KJ64 would be an attacking lead, working well if partner produced the ace or queen, otherwise risking giving declarer a free trick.

A passive lead is more defensive, a safe lead which leaves declarer to do his own work. Leading a trump, or any suit like three or four small, qualifies. Holdings such as KQJ are ideal because they are both active and safe.

The bidding gives you a clue. Suppose your opponents struggle into game, sounding as though they have nothing to spare. Now is the time to go passive making declarer have to work hard. Look at these bidding sequences:

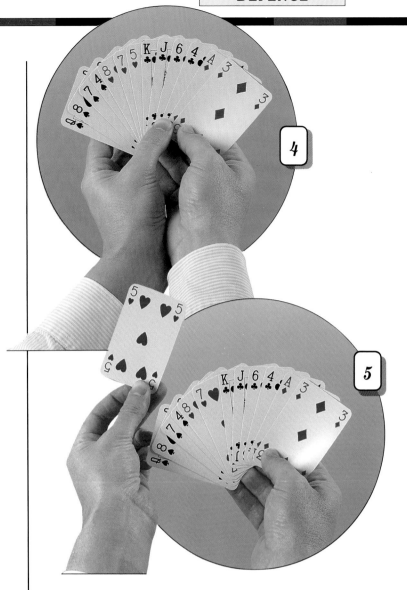

(i)	1♡—2♡	(ii)	1NT—2NT	(iii)	1♠—2♣
	3♡—4♡		3NT—Pass		2♠—3♠
	Pass				4♠—Pass

All these sequences suggest declarer has nothing to spare. Conversely, when your opponents bounce into game, or when things sound to be lying well for them (dummy has bid the suits where you hold strength), now you should attack, as declarer will surely succeed if left to himself.

(iv)	1♠—2♣	(v)	1♠—3♢	(vi)	1♡—2♣
	3♢—4♠		3♠—4♠		2NT—4♡
	Pass		Pass		Pass

All these are strong sequences. If you make an attacking lead and it gives away a trick, it is likely only to be an overtrick – not so important. The thing to avoid is giving away the vital contract-making trick, and that is more a danger when your opponents sound weaker, hence that is the time to play safe.

The auction goes:

1♡—Pass—3♡—Pass
4♡—All Pass

and you have to lead from these holdings (**3, 4**). What should you do?

(**3**) You should lead ♠Q. This is both active and safe. It may establish tricks for your side but cannot give declarer anything he could not do for himself.

A club lead would also be safe but not at all active, while a heart is fairly safe and reduces declarer's ruffing potential. A diamond would be very active and very dangerous, though it could work brilliantly if partner has the ace.

(**4**) Lead a trump (**5**). Any side suit is a stab in the dark, great if you hit partner's strength and potentially disastrous otherwise. A low club is next best. Dangerous because from a broken holding, but needing only ace or queen from partner to be good.

A spade needs two honours from partner to be good so is less likely to work but is still dangerous, while a diamond risks declarer making the king when he should not do so.

QUIZ ON OPENING LEADS

In each case (**1-4**), what should you lead on the given auctions?

(A)

S	W	N	E
–	–	–	1NT
Pass	3NT	All Pass	

♣6. Try to establish some extra tricks by leading from your five-card suit.

(B)

S	W	N	E
–	–	–	1♡
Pass	2♢	Pass	3♡
Pass	4♡	All Pass	

♠K. Your opponents have bid confidently to game and both their suits seem to be lying very favourably for them. Time for desperate measures and an attacking lead. Maybe partner has the ace.

(C)

S	W	N	E
–	–	–	1♠
Pass	3♠	Pass	4♠
All Pass			

♡10. Anything else would be a big gamble. There is nothing in the auction to suggest you should do other than lead your sequence.

(D)

S	W	N	E
–	–	–	1♣
Pass	1♡	Pass	1♠
Pass	3♡	Pass	3NT
All Pass			

3♢. Declarer has bid your long suit and dummy your sequence. Try the unbid suit and hope partner has both length and strength there.

(E)

S	W	N	E
–	–	–	1NT
Pass	2NT	Pass	3NT
All Pass			

♢10. They have scraped into game with no long suits and no spare values, so look no further than your sequence – the safest lead.

(F)

S	W	N	E
–	1♢	1♡	1NT
Pass	2NT	All Pass	

♡3. When partner bids a suit, you need a very good alternative before you look elsewhere for your opening lead. Just as in any other suit, you should lead low from an honour.

(G)

S	W	N	E
–	–	–	1♠
Pass	2♠	Pass	3♠
Pass	4♠	All Pass	

♠4. Your opponents have bid game on minimal values. Declarer may need to ruff losers in dummy so a trump lead looks best. Though it is not so important, traditionally the lead from three low trumps is the middle one (and low from two small).

(H)

S	W	N	E
–	1♡	Pass	1♠
Pass	3♡	Pass	3♠
Pass	4♠	All Pass	

♣4. Time for an attacking lead, because it looks as though dummy has a long strong suit on which declarer will be able to throw his losers if given time to do so.

Now for the next example (**3**).

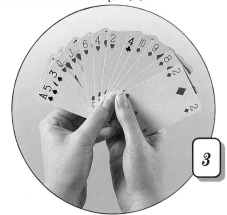

(I)	S	W	N	E
–	–	–	1NT
Pass	3NT	All Pass

♡4. With a fair five-card suit and an outside entry, lead fourth best of your long suit.

(J)	S	W	N	E
–	1♡	Pass	1NT
Pass	3NT	All Pass

◇10. As an opponent has bid your long suit, it seems partner will not have the help you need in hearts. Instead, try your second suit – which also happens to feature a nice safe sequence.

(K)	S	W	N	E
–	–	–	1♠
Pass	3♠	Pass	4♠
All Pass		

♣4. A diamond lead would be safe, but a club is much more likely to beat the contract. If partner has the ♣A he can win and give you a club ruff immediately. If not, you can try to find an entry to his hand when you win your trump ace.

(L)	S	W	N	E
–	1♣	1♠	1NT
2♠	3NT	All Pass

♠3. You have a fair suit of your own but when partner has bid and you have help in his suit, you need a *very* good reason not to lead it.

Finally, look at this hand (**4**).

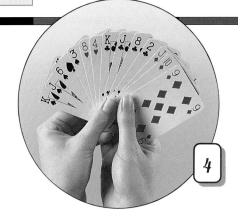

(M)	S	W	N	E
–	–	–	1♠
Pass	2♡	Pass	2NT
Pass	3NT	All Pass

◇J. You have a good holding sitting over declarer's suit and can hope that partner is similarly placed over dummy's hearts. As declarer may be going to struggle, choose a safe lead.

(N)	S	W	N	E
–	–	–	1♡
Pass	1♠	Pass	1NT
Pass	3NT	All Pass

♣2. This time the majors both appear to be well placed for declarer, so your only hope of defeating 3NT seems to be to attack by leading your longest suit and hope to establish some tricks there.

(O)	S	W	N	E
–	–	–	1♡
Pass	2◇	Pass	2♠
Pass	3♡	Pass	4♡
All Pass		

♡4. Declarer has shown a strong hand by reversing into spades, but your spade holding suggests you may have a chance, but only if you can stop declarer from trumping his spade losers in the dummy.

(P)	S	W	N	E
–	–	–	1♡
Pass	2♣	Pass	2◇
Pass	3♡	Pass	4♡
All Pass		

♠3. The bidding suggests that three suits are lying well for declarer, meaning that given time he is likely to succeed in making his contract. In that case we need to attack.

GENERAL RULES OF DEFENCE

When partner leads the first card to a trick, it is your responsibility (playing third) to do the best you can to try and win the trick. Take this layout (**1**). Say that West leads the two. If you play the ten, not wanting to "waste" your king, declarer scoops in a cheap trick with his jack and still has the ace left as a second trick.

Now suppose you play the king to the first trick (**2**). True, your king is doomed to lose to declarer's ace, but when you gain the lead in another suit you can lead through declarer's remaining J7, trapping the jack and holding him to only one trick in the suit.

This is a quite different situation (**3**). If West leads the two and dummy plays small, the way to restrict declarer to only one trick is to play your ten (**4**). The king would lose to the ace and leave dummy's jack as an eventual second trick for declarer. Here, you have to *finesse* against a card (the jack) in the dummy. If there is no high card in dummy, always try your best as in the first example.

Where you have two or more touching cards, always play the lowest one which will do the job. For example, you hold QJ4 and partner leads the two. Play the jack. Say this is the layout (**5**).

When the jack forces the ace (**6**), your partner will know you also hold the queen, otherwise declarer would have won with that card. Suppose instead that you held only Q94 and therefore played the queen. When this loses to the ace, partner knows declarer has the jack because you would have played the jack from queen-jack. Sticking to rules like this helps partner to place the missing high cards and plan an effective defence.

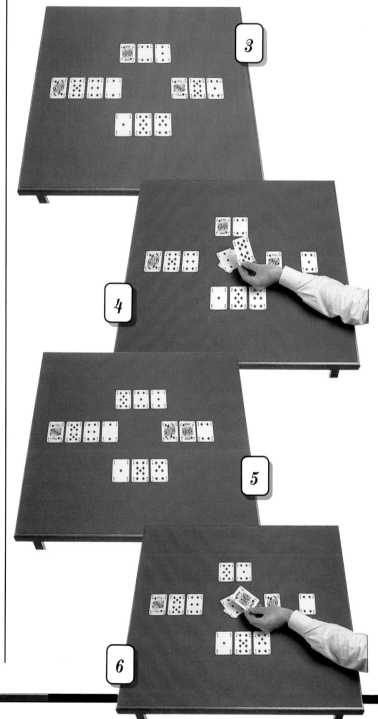

SECOND HAND PLAY

We have seen that third hand should usually play high, trying to win the trick. What about second hand, where either declarer or dummy has led to the trick? Where you have two or more touching honour cards, it is often a good idea to play one of them. For example, you hold KQ3 and declarer leads low towards dummy's AJ4. If you do not play the queen or king, declarer may insert dummy's jack and make a cheap trick.

Otherwise, however, the general rule is for second hand to play low unless the lead was an honour. Take this layout (**7**). If declarer leads the two and you put up the king he has three easy tricks. If you play low (**8**), dummy's jack wins but you still hold the king ready to beat the queen and he gets only two tricks.

Suppose declarer leads an honour. If it is unsupported, i.e. you can see no other honour backing it up, you should generally cover. In this situation (**9**) if dummy leads the queen and you play low, declarer plays his nine then leads the suit again, intending to finesse his jack. He scores three tricks. If you play the king on the queen (**10**), it is beaten by the ace but partner's ten comes into its own on the second or third round of the suit.

If you can see a sequence of honours, it is best not to cover until the last one is led. If the queen is led in this situation (**11**) and you cover, declarer wins the

ace and can then lead towards the J9, finessing against partner's ten. If you duck the queen (**12**), then cover if declarer continues with the jack, you promote partner's ten into a trick.

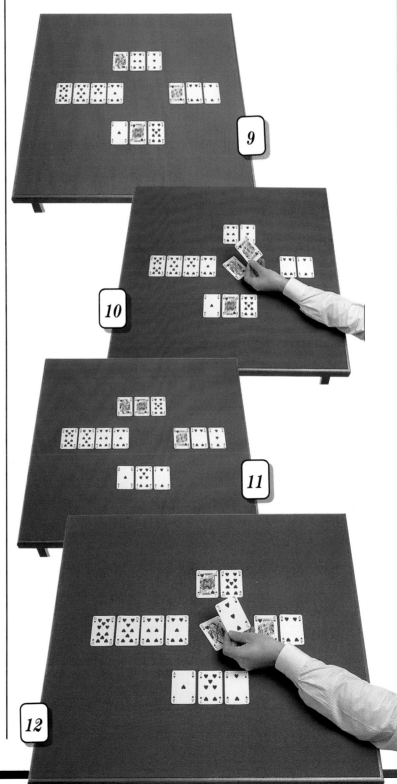

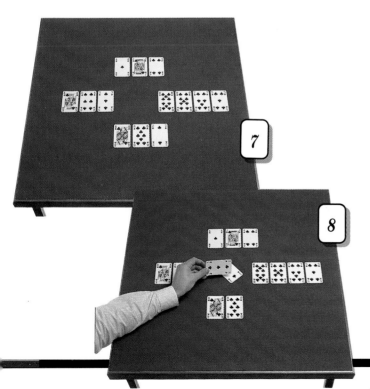

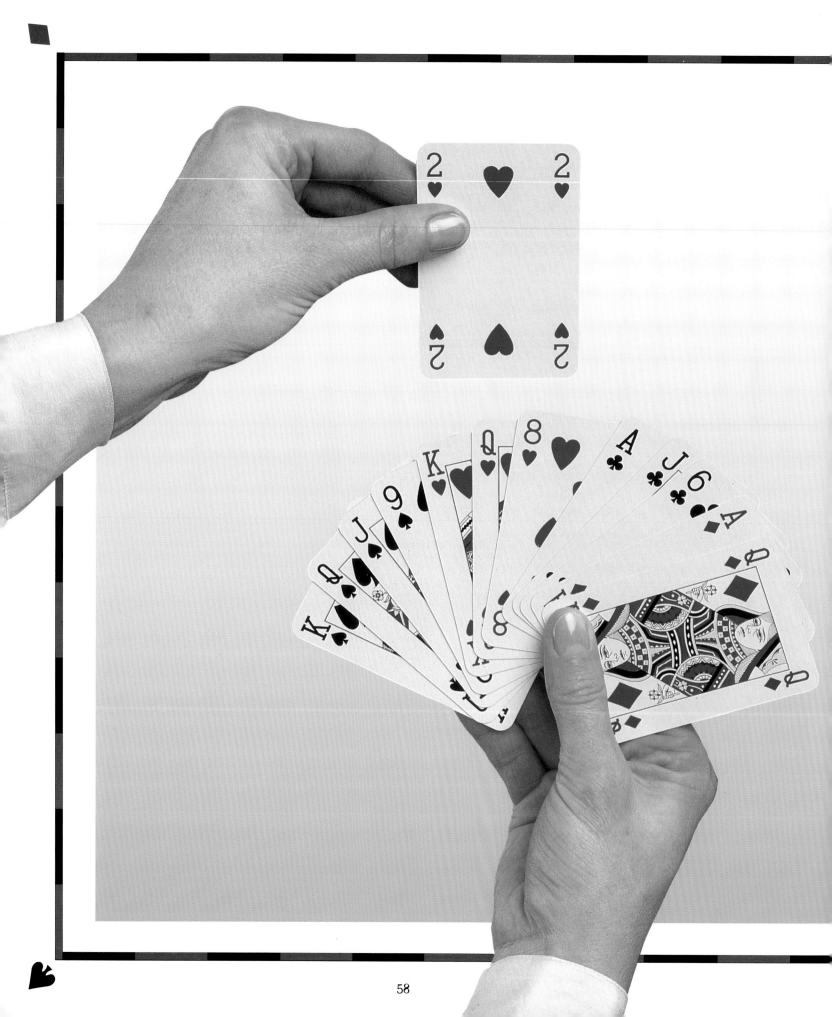

PART TWO

BUILDING ON THE BASICS

COMPETITIVE BIDDING

The opposition open one of a suit. What should you do? So far the opposition have stayed conveniently quiet, but of course in real life that will frequently not be the case. A lot of points can be won and lost in competitive auctions. When an opponent opens the bidding, you are in a quite different situation from when you are first to speak, and some of the rules of bidding you have so painstakingly learned need to be modified. Partly, this is because it has become more dangerous to bid now that one opponent already knows his partner has a good hand. Also, some bids have been taken away from you. If your right-hand opponent opens 1♡, it is no longer possible for you to bid 1♣, 1♢ or 1♡. A new scheme is required to cater for the new circumstances you find yourself in.

There are four different types of bid you can make when an opponent opens one of a suit.

AN OVERCALL IN A NEW SUIT

If you bid a new suit over an opponent's opening bid you are making what is called an **overcall**. At the one level, an overcall promises a decent five-card or longer suit and about 8-15 HCP. To overcall at the two level promises a little more, as you might expect when you take the bidding to a higher level, roughly 11-15 HCP and a good five-card suit or better. Over a 1♢ opening, bid 1♠ on either (**1**) or (**2**).

However, bid 2♣ on (**3**) but pass with (**4**) which does not justify a bid at the two level.

You should always have a reasonable suit as partner will naturally lead it if you end up in defence and also the opponents will find it much more difficult to penalize you if you pick the wrong moment to come in to the auction. An overcall tells partner you have a distinct preference for one suit over all the others.

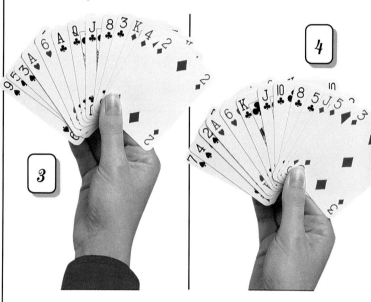

THE JUMP OVERCALL

A **jump overcall** is exactly what it sounds like: a jump in a new suit. Over a 1♡ opening, 2♠, 3♣ and 3♢ are the jump overcalls. It shows a single-suited hand with at least a strong six-card suit and about 12-16 HCP. Over a 1♡ opening, these would be typical examples of 2♠ and 3♢ bids respectively (**5, 6**).

THE ONE NO TRUMP OVERCALL

A 1NT overcall shows a balanced hand of 15-17HCP (though some players prefer 16-18), just like a 1NT opening bid. However, one important difference is that you must have a stopper in the opponents' suit, i.e. at least one trick in it. After all, that is the suit they are likely to lead and it would be very awkward if you lost the first five or six tricks before you even gained the lead. Over a 1♡ opening, bid 1NT with (**7**) but find an alternative with (**8**).

THE TAKEOUT DOUBLE

Bidding hand (**8**) above is solved by use of something called a **takeout double**. When an opponent opens one of a suit, the chance that you will be both long and strong enough in the same suit to want to double him for penalties is extremely remote. Instead, the double is used to say "Partner I am strong enough to want to bid but have no obvious bid to make. Would you pick a suit please?" This takeout double shows at least the strength to open the bidding, had you had the chance to do so, and support for all the other three suits. The longer you are in opener's suit, the less support you will have for the other suits, so the more high card strength you need to compensate. These three examples are all roughly minimum takeout doubles of a 1♡ opening (**9**).

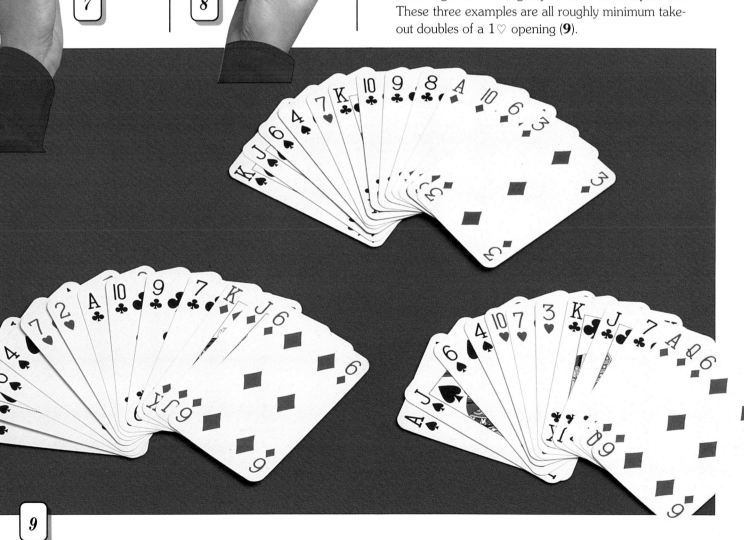

RESPONDING TO OVERCALLS

Wen partner overcalls, you may bid with as few as six points if you have support for his suit. It is not so much that you expect to make game your way when you are so weak, as that you do not know to which side the deal really belongs so want to make life difficult for your opponents.

SIMPLE SUIT OVERCALLS

As partner has promised a five-card suit, you can raise freely with three-card support. A simple raise shows about 6-10 points, a jump raise 11-13, and a raise to game 14+. The last of these should really include four-card support unless you have extra points, say 16+ if only three trumps.

If the bidding begins 1♣ – 1♠ – Pass – ?, what should you bid with these hands (**1-3**)?

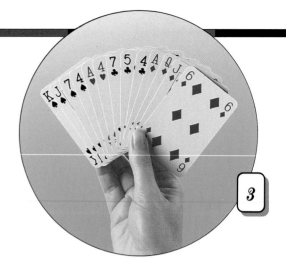

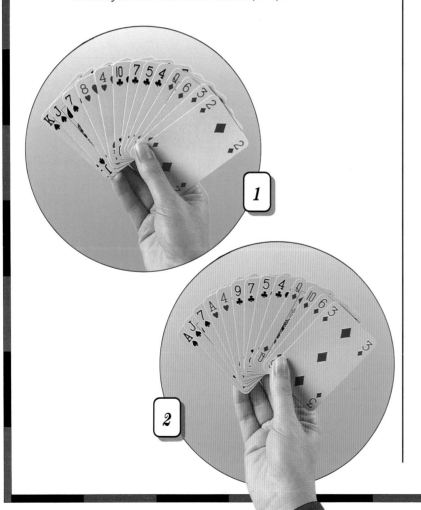

Bid 2♠ with (**1**), 3♠ with (**2**), and 4♠ with (**3**). If you do not have support for partner there is no reason to bid with less than nine or ten points. As he is limited to at most fifteen, with no trump fit game is unlikely. So you will pass with a number of hands with which you would have responded to an opening bid.

If you do decide to respond, you may either bid No Trumps or a new suit. A bid in a new suit should guarantee at least five cards. It is not forcing but it is constructive. In other words, partner can pass but should bid again with a good hand or a fit for your suit. If you want to force him to bid again you can always jump in your suit to show a very good hand.

A bid in No Trumps is, as always, a limit bid. You must bid the full value of your hand immediately. Opposite a one level overcall:

1NT = 9-11 HCP
2NT = 12-14 HCP
3NT = 15+ HCP

Opposite a two level overcall:

2NT = 10-12 HCP
3NT = 13+ HCP

In all cases it is absolutely essential that you have at least one stopper in the opponents' suit as that is the one they will normally lead. It is no use having ten tricks to take in 3NT if you lose the first five.

If the bidding goes 1♣ – 1♡ – Pass – ?, what should you bid with these hands (**4-6**)?

With (**4**), pass as there is little likelihood of game opposite at most 15 HCP. Bid 1♠ with (**5**), five plus cards and constructive but non-forcing. (**6**) is a perfect 1NT bid, a balanced ten points with a solid stopper in their suit.

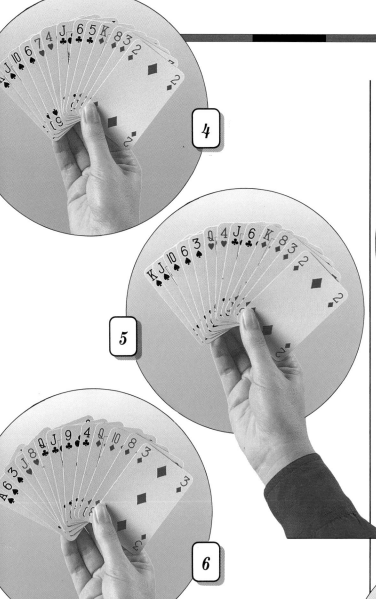

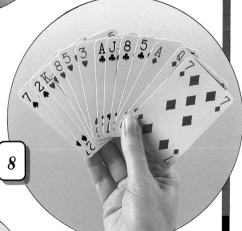

1♣ – 2♠ – Pass – ? What would your bid now be with these hands (**7-9**)?

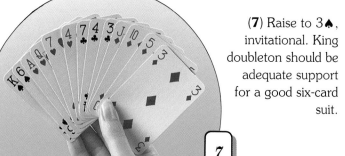

(**7**) Raise to 3♠, invitational. King doubleton should be adequate support for a good six-card suit.

(**8**) Bid 3NT. You have doubleton support but have strength in all the other suits and a balanced hand, so nine tricks may be easier than ten.

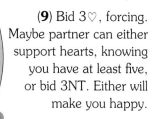

(**9**) Bid 3♡, forcing. Maybe partner can either support hearts, knowing you have at least five, or bid 3NT. Either will make you happy.

JUMP OVERCALLS

Partner has shown 12-16 HCP and a very strong preference for his suit. If you decide to bid you will usually either raise his suit or bid No Trumps. After all, facing a good six-card suit you can raise with as little as a doubleton and still be sure of an eight-card fit, can't you? If you do bid a new suit, it should be a forcing bid as otherwise you could be really stuck with a good hand with simply no room to force by jumping in a new suit.

A simple raise of partner's suit or a bid of 2NT should be around 8-10 points and is invitational, while you should jump to game with 11+ points. As always, to bid No Trumps you must have a stopper in the opponents' suit.

ONE NO TRUMP OVERALL

The rules for bidding opposite a 1NT overcall are exactly the same as those for bidding opposite a 1NT opening bid.

RESPONDING TO TAKEOUT DOUBLES

If the third player passes, you must respond to a takeout double even with nothing. It may sound risky but the alternative is far worse as if you pass they will almost certainly make their doubled contract, probably with overtricks. Remember, partner is usually short in their suit so if you are weak where will you find the tricks to beat them?

The idea of the takeout double is to ask you to choose a trump suit, but you should also tell partner if you have a good hand or are merely bidding because he forced you to do so. The way to show a reasonable hand is to jump. For example, here is the scheme after 1◇ – Double – Pass – ?

1♡/1♠/2♣ = 0-8 points and your longest suit. With two equal suits bid the cheaper of the four-card suits, the higher of five-card suits, just as when opening or responding to an opening. So bid 1♠ with:

- ♠ 10863
- ♡ 974
- ◇ Q3
- ♣ QJ74

2♡/2♠/3♣ = 9-12 points and your longest suit. Bid 2♡ with:

- ♠ A6
- ♡ AQ74
- ◇ 9753
- ♣ 1097

1NT = 6-10 points and a balanced hand with at least one stopper in their suit, e.g.

- ♠ K63
- ♡ J104
- ◇ KJ73
- ♣ 1092

2NT = 11-12 points, a good stopper and a balanced hand, e.g.

- ♠ K65
- ♡ 1097
- ◇ AJ10
- ♣ QJ74

Pass = Very rare. You need very long and strong trumps and a positive desire to defend; you are not just passing out of weakness, e.g.

- ♠ 742
- ♡ K6
- ◇ KQJ98
- ♣ 853

None of the above bids is forcing, though if the doubler thinks game is possible given the strength you have shown (or denied), he should bid again. When partner doubles and you have 13+ points you should want to play in game. There are two ways to achieve this. The obvious one is simply to jump to game in your suit or in No Trumps. To do this in a suit you need five, as partner will not always have four-card support, while to bid 3NT you need at least one and preferably two stoppers in their suit.

After 1◇ – Double – Pass – ?, what should you bid with these hands (**1-3**)?

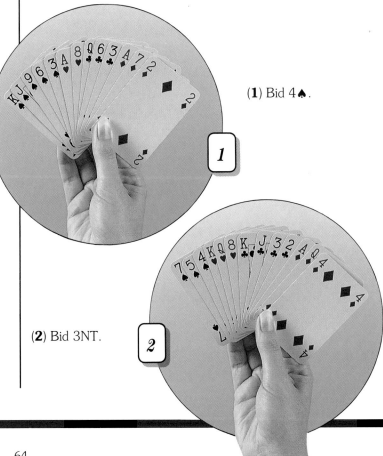

(**1**) Bid 4♠.

(**2**) Bid 3NT.

(**3**) is a problem, game values but no five-card suit and only a single stopper. Here you should **cuebid,** as explained below.

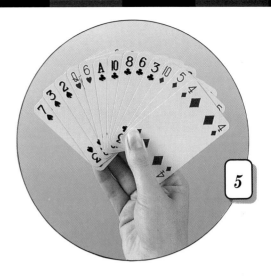

It may look strange but the answer to (**3**) is to **cue-bid** the opponents' suit. Diamonds is the one suit you cannot wish to play in – if you did you would just pass one diamond doubled – so a bid of 2◇, known as a cuebid, says '"Partner, I want to play in game but don't know which one; please help".

After the cuebid, each player bids his or her suits in turn, longest first, until a fit is found or possibly 3NT is reached. Here, instead of guessing between 3NT/4♡/4♠, you can explore properly. If you have a 4-4 fit you will find it, if not you can get to 3NT.

THIRD HAND BIDS

If the third hand bids, (e.g. 1◇ – Double – 1♠), you are relieved of the obligation to respond to the dou-ble. That does not mean you should automatically pass. If you are weak, by all means take advantage of the opportunity to say so, but with something worth showing, make the same bid as you would normally have done. Look at these hands (**4, 5**).

With (**4**), by all means Pass, but you are not ashamed of (**5**) and should bid 2♣. Partner will not get carried away as you are limited to at most eight points. Add, say, the ♠K and you would jump to 3♣.

THE DOUBLER BIDS A NEW SUIT

One advantage of the takeout double is that you force partner to speak, so will get another chance to bid. What do you make of this auction?

Partner	You
1◇ Double	Pass 1♠
Pass 2♡	

Why did he ask your opinion and then overrule you? Partner must have at least five hearts to bid this way so could have overcalled. The best explanation is that he was too strong to overcall, holding perhaps this hand (**6**). So to double, then bid a new suit shows 16+ HCP and a good suit. It is not forcing but it is highly encouraging. With an even stronger hand, the dou-bler could jump in his suit.

BIDDING AGAINST NO TRUMP OPENINGS

When your right-hand opponent opens 1NT he makes a very precise bid, telling his partner both that he is balanced and what his strength is within very narrow limits. If you intervene, his partner is very well placed to know what to do as he has an excellent picture of his side's combined assets. In particular, if you overcall and he has a few of your suit plus some strength, he is well placed to make a penalty double and sometimes extract a painfully large penalty from you.

When an opponent opens 1NT, you should only overcall if you have a six-card suit or, if only five, a very strong suit or possibly a hand with some outside shape which might be useful in the play. 5-3-3-2 is a very poor shape, with no long sidesuit to establish and little opportunity to ruff anything. 5-4-3-1 or, better, 5-5-2-1 gives much more scope in the play.

I do not want to put you off overcalling altogether. True, the odd −800 points is a spectacularly bad result, but repeatedly passing and letting your opponents make 1NT when you could have bid and made 2♡ can be just as expensive in the long run. Take a look at these hands (**1-3**).

Hand (**1**) should pass over a 1NT opening; the spade suit is adequate but the shape horrible and you could have a lot of losers if you bid at the wrong time. Lead a spade and hope partner has enough help to beat 1NT.

The sixth spade makes (**2**) worth an overcall. Not only do you have one more likely trick in your hand, it is also one less spade an opponent can hold, making a double less likely. Though hand (**3**) has only five spades, it is worth a bid because the useful diamond suit and singleton give extra playing strength. This hand rates to make a trick or two more than hand (**1**) most of the time.

When partner overcalls, you should assume he has something similar to a hand allowing an overcall at the two level after a one of a suit opening and bid accordingly.

If you do not have a long suit to overcall, you have two choices, either to pass or to double. It does not make sense for a double to be takeout here – what suit are you taking out of? Instead, a double is basically for penalties, showing a fairly balanced hand which is stronger than the 1NT opener. Assuming 1NT showed 15-17 – worth checking as some people play differently – these are both good doubles (**4, 5**).

(**4**) has 18 HCP, comfortably more than the opener, and if partner has his fair share of what little is left, you can hope to beat 1NT quite comfortably.

Hand (**5**) has only 16 HCP and your instinct might be to overcall 2♠. Think, however, that you have six tricks in your hand so need very little help to beat 1NT, and if partner has a good hand you might collect a very nice penalty indeed.

When partner doubles 1NT and the next hand passes, he normally expects you to pass. There are two sorts of hand with which you might bid. One is a very weak hand with which you fear that one No Trump doubled will make. Now you might run to two of your longest suit. The other is a good hand with a very long suit. In this case you are afraid that you have game on and that the penalty from one No Trump doubled will be inadequate compensation, particularly as partner will never guess to lead your suit. This time you should jump to game in your suit.

After 1NT – Double – Pass – ?, how would you bid on these hands (**6-8**)?

Hand (**6**) should pass. If partner has a minimum double, you may not beat 1NT. But you have no guarantee that anything else will be better – if you bid

2♡ partner may have only a doubleton on a bad day. Best is to pass and hope he has a little more than a minimum double and your bits and pieces will be enough to scramble seven tricks. With (**7**) you are even weaker. Beating 1NT looks very unlikely and this time you have a five-card suit to bid. 2◇ looks to be the bid, just as you would have done had partner opened 1NT.

(**8**) is an example of a hand which expects to make game opposite a hand which can double 1NT. Jump to 4♡; if you bid less, partner may pass.

DECLARER PLAY – PLANNING

I said earlier that declarer should always try to make a plan before starting to play. She should start by counting her top tricks, then look at each suit in turn to see where the extra tricks needed to fulfil the contract might come from. She needs to work out what order to play the suits in, making sure that she has all the necessary communications between the two hands, and she has to look for any possible problems. Sometimes, if she can recognize a possible problem before she reaches it, declarer can find a way to overcome it. What chance does she have if she does not even know the problem exists?

South plays in 3NT on the lead of the ♠K in this hand (**1**). How should she play? First she counts her tricks – one spade, four hearts and three diamonds. Where can the ninth trick be found? The only possibility is the ♣K and the best chance of success is to lead low from dummy towards the king, hoping that East holds the ace.

Any more problems? Well, the hearts are blocked. Declarer must cash the ace, king and queen before crossing to dummy's sole entry (♢K). Then she must cash ♡J and lead towards the club.

There is still one more problem. What if West has five spades and East the ♣A? Declarer must duck two rounds of spades and only win the third round. Now East has no spade left to lead when she wins the ♣A. This is how the whole deal looks (**2**).

PLAY SUMMARY BOX

TRICK												
1	**2**	**3**	**4**	**5**	**6**	**7**	**8**	**9**	**10**	**11**	**12**	**13**
W	W	W	S	S	S	S	N	N	S	S	S	E
♠K	♠Q	♠J	♡A	♡K	♡Q	♢4	♡J	♣4	♢A	♢Q	♣6	♣J
N	N	N	W	W	W	W	E	E	W	W	W	S
♠2	♠7	♣2	♡2	♡10	♢2	♢5	♡9	♣9	♢10	♠5	♣Q	♠8
E	E	E	N	N	N	N	S	S	N	N	N	W
♠3	♠4	♠9	♡4	♡6	♡8	♢K	♣3	♣K	♢3	♢8	♣7	♠10
S	S	S	E	E	E	E	W	W	E	E	E	N
♠6	♠8	♠A	♡3	♡5	♡7	♢6	♢7	♣5	♢9	♢J	♣A	♣10

Try it again if South fails to duck the first two spades. Now East wins the first club and returns a spade – one down.

In this example (**3**) South plays in 4♠ on the lead of the ◇K. There are only six top tricks but declarer can see either three or four extra tricks in spades plus a chance of making the ♡Q. Her plan is to finesse in spades, hoping that East has the king and it can be trapped. Her hope in hearts is also that East has the king.

The best play is to win the ◇A and lead the ♠J, running it if East plays low. If the jack wins, repeat the finesse and draw trumps. If the spade loses, win as soon as you can, draw the missing trumps and play ♡A and low to the ♡Q. 4♠ makes if East has either major suit king – about a 75 percent chance.

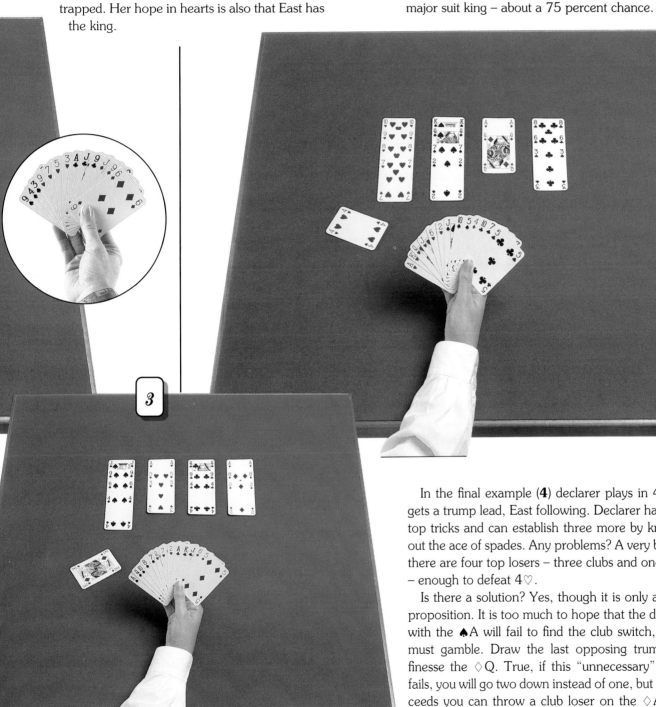

In the final example (**4**) declarer plays in 4♡ and gets a trump lead, East following. Declarer has seven top tricks and can establish three more by knocking out the ace of spades. Any problems? A very big one; there are four top losers – three clubs and one spade – enough to defeat 4♡.

Is there a solution? Yes, though it is only a 50-50 proposition. It is too much to hope that the defender with the ♠A will fail to find the club switch, so you must gamble. Draw the last opposing trump, and finesse the ◇Q. True, if this "unnecessary" finesse fails, you will go two down instead of one, but if it succeeds you can throw a club loser on the ◇A. With only three top losers, now you can afford to set about spades.

DUCKING

The first example of planning the play as declarer, shown on page 68, featured a very important technique – the ducking play. One use of this technique is to preserve your own communications.

For example, in this hand (**1**) West leads ◇A against 4♠ then switches to a trump. Without the trump switch, declarer could have hoped to ruff her third diamond in dummy to provide the tenth trick. Clearly the defence will not allow this. If she plays a second diamond, they will win and play a second trump.

What is the alternative? The only possible tenth trick must come from clubs, a 3-3 break meaning that North's fourth card can be established. Correct play in 4♠ is to win the trump switch and play a low club from each hand (a ducking play). When you regain the lead you can draw the outstanding trumps and play ♣K and a club to the ace. If clubs were 3-3 originally dummy will be on lead and can cash the thirteenth club to give ten tricks.

More often, ducking plays are designed to cut your opponents' communications. Suppose West leads the ♠Q against 3NT in this deal (**2**). Declarer has eight top tricks and the ninth can only come from diamonds. Say she wins the first spade and leads a diamond. East wins the ace and returns her last spade.

West forces out declarer's second spade stopper and has three winners to cash when he wins the next diamond – one down.

Now try it if West is allowed to win the first trick. He plays a second spade but this time East has no spade left to lead when she wins the ◇A. With only one entry, West can establish his winners but never gets the lead to cash them.

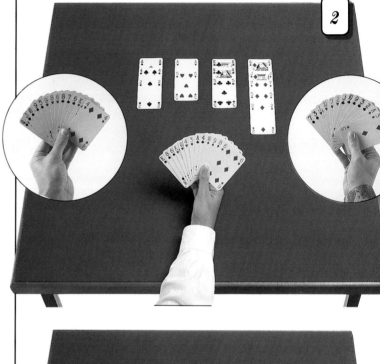

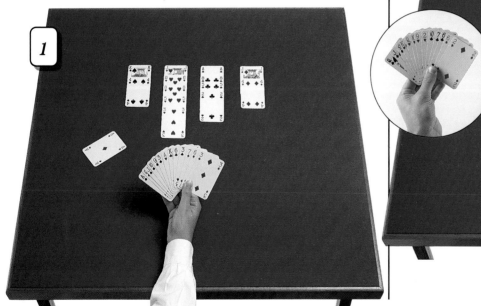

4

Now in this deal (**3**), West leads the ♡K against 3NT. Declarer needs extra tricks from diamonds and will normally try the finesse. Suppose she wins the first heart and runs the ◇Q. This loses to the king and back comes a heart through her jack. West cashes four hearts – one down.

If declarer ducks the first heart, West is powerless. A second heart would give declarer an extra trick there while declarer can win any switch quite happily and take the diamond finesse. Again, the duck brings home the contract. This particular duck, with AJx(x) is known as The Bath Coup.

While ducking is a valuable technique it is important to know when not to use it. Look at this deal (**4**). West leads ♠5 against 3NT. Say declarer plays low from dummy. East wins the queen and returns ♠6. Seeing dummy's bare ace, West does not waste one of his honours. With only eight winners, declarer must establish a diamond trick but West wins the first diamond and cashes three spades – one down.

A thinking declarer will realize that West would not lead low from KQJ. A 4-3 break is no problem as there can only be three spade losers, but a 5-2 break where East has doubleton honour is dangerous.

Rising with the ace at trick one blocks the suit, leaving the spade holding split as shown (**5**). When West wins ◇A, how is he to cash all the spades now?

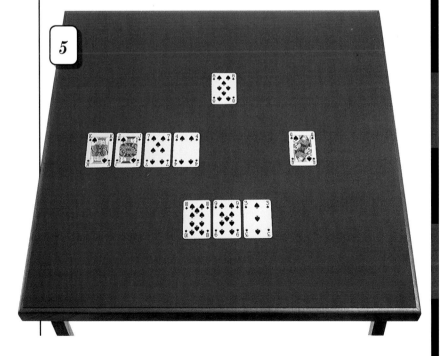

5

COUNTING

Bridge does not require any higher mathematics, but it does help if you learn to count. When planning the play, you need to be able to count your winners and losers. During the play, what might otherwise be a complete guess can often be turned into a sure thing by counting points – the high cards each defender turns up with – and cards – the number of each suit played by each defender.

Let me be honest, counting will not come easily at first – you just have so much else to think about when you first start to play bridge. However, if you persevere, always trying to keep track of what cards have been played and by whom, it will get easier and the information you can gain will be so valuable that it is well worth the effort.

In this situation (**1**) West leads a club against 3NT. Declarer can count seven top tricks and can establish two more by playing on diamonds – no problem.

How about the same contract on a heart lead? The problem is that the defence is a step ahead. To establish their suit they need to knock out the ace and king of hearts. For declarer to establish her suit she has to knock out the ace and king of diamonds. But the defence will get there first and as one of them must have at least five hearts, they will have five winners.

If declarer thinks about this *before* she starts to play, she can look for an alternative. Instead of playing on diamonds she should gamble on the spade finesse. If West holds the king she can make three spades, two hearts and four clubs – nine in all. Check this by studying the complete hand (**2**).

In this example (**3**) South plays 4♡ after West has opened 1NT. West leads ♣Q to the king and ace and East plays the ace, king and queen of diamonds. Dummy ruffs the third diamond and declarer draws trumps. Her problem is a simple one: who has the missing ♠Q? The answer lies in the bidding. East opened 1NT and has shown up with 13 points – ♣A, ◇AKQ to West's three – ♣QJ. Only the ♠Q is unaccounted for. If East/West are playing a strong No Trump (15-17), East must have the queen for her opening bid. Careful though, some people play a weak No Trump (12-14). If your opponents have this agreement, then East cannot have the ♠Q as this would give her too much to open 1NT.

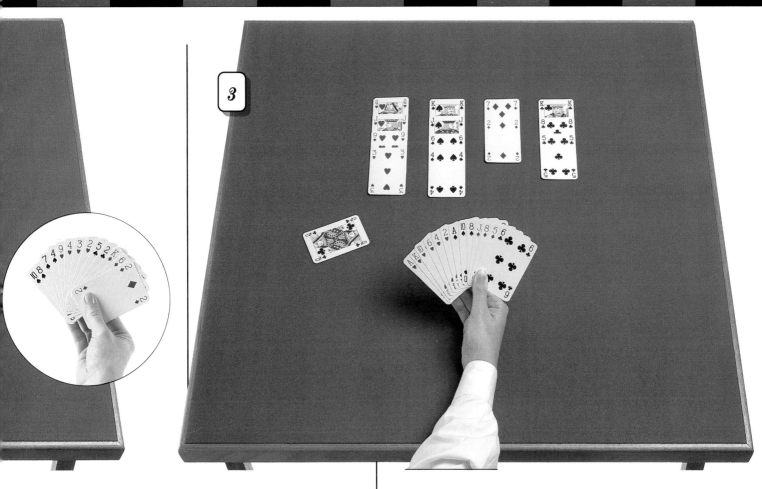

Here (**4**) South is declarer in 7NT on the ♠9 lead. She seems to have a complete guess as to the whereabouts of the ♣Q. With so much at stake it is worth delaying the decision as long as possible. Perhaps cashing all the winners in the other suits will give a clue as to how to play the clubs.

Whoever is long in one suit is more likely to be short in another. Suppose that West follows to all three rounds of spades while East discards a heart on the third round. The same thing happens in diamonds, West follows three times while East discards a heart on the third one. Now cash the hearts. This time East follows three times while West discards a diamond on the last one. Would you believe that the contract is now a sure thing?

We know that West has 5 spades, 5 diamonds, 2 hearts and therefore 1 club

East has 2 spades, 2 diamonds, 5 hearts and therefore 4 clubs. Play ♣K and see West's only club. Now lead ♣J and know that the club finesse is bound to succeed – West cannot have any club, let alone the queen.

COMPETITIVE BIDDING – THE OPPONENTS OVERCALL

An overcall by one of your opponents does not make a huge difference to how you bid but there are three significant changes to bear in mind.

Firstly, if an opponent bids a suit you must never be the first member of your partnership to bid No Trumps unless you have a solid stopper in that suit. The overcaller has promised a decent five-card suit and that is the suit they are likely to lead. Obviously, you would not like to lose five or six tricks before you even gained the lead.

Secondly, while you are expected to find some response to a suit opening whenever you have six or more points in an uncontested auction, once they intervene you are allowed to pass if you have nothing you want to say. After all, partner is going to get another chance if he wants one whether or not you bid. Sometimes, you will have no option but to pass with six plus points. After 1◇ – 1♠ – ?, how should you bid with this hand?

- ♠ 1063
- ♡ Q8742
- ◇ K7
- ♣ J104

You are not strong enough to bid a new suit at the two level, cannot support diamonds, and cannot bid No Trumps with no spade stopper. That only leaves Pass. However, after 1◇ – 1♡ – ?, bid 1♠ on:

- ♠ Q8742
- ♡ 1063
- ◇ K7
- ♣ J104

because you are strong enough to bid a new suit at the one level.

The third change is that you have an extra option, namely to double. When your side has already made a positive bid in the auction, a double is for penalties. It shows both strength and considerable length in the overcaller's suit plus some outside strength, and you hope to get him several down for a big penalty. After 1♣ – 1♡ –? what should you bid here?

- ♠ J64
- ♡ KQ1083
- ◇ AJ4
- ♣ 72

Double for penalties. Partner will usually pass your penalty doubles. If he does bid it is because he has an exceptionally distributional hand where he is very keen to make one of his suits trumps.

Now look at these hands (**1-3**). After 1♣ – 1♡ – Double – Pass –?, what should you bid?

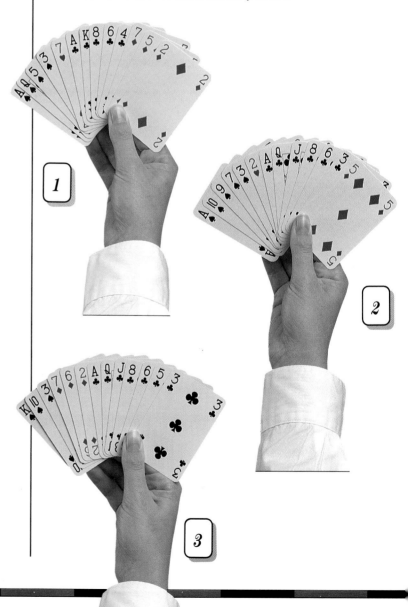

74

Pass with (**1**). You have a second suit but your shape is nothing special. Hand (**2**) should bid 1♠. When partner doubled he did not imagine you had such a two-suited hand. Hand (**3**) should bid 2♣, because of the exceptional length of the suit and low point count. Defending one heart doubled will often be a struggle.

When the opponents overcall with 1NT, a double is for penalties and promises your side has the balance of the points, so should be at least nine or ten points. A bid in a new suit is not forcing, showing at least five cards but not enough to double.

QUIZ HANDS

The bidding goes 1◇ – 1♠ – ? What is your next bid with these hands (**4-7**)?

Double. The spades should produce four tricks in defence while your shortage in partner's suit will make it that much harder to find a good contract your way (**7**).

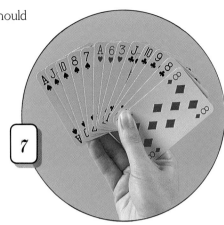

1NT. As you have a spade stopper you can afford to bid 1NT, showing a balanced 6-9 HCP (**4**).

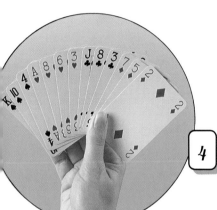

2♡. Ten points and a decent five-card suit is worth a two over one response (**5**).

Now look at hands (**8,9**), what is your next bid if the auction begins 1♡ – 2♣ – ?

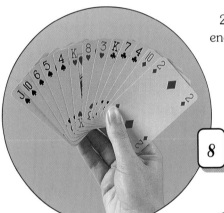

2♡. You are not strong enough for 2♠ but would like to bid something. To raise partner with three to an honour is acceptable when the alternative is to say nothing (**8**).

3◇. Just as you would have bid without the overcall (**6**).

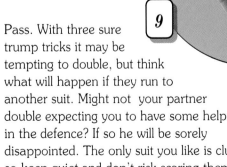

Pass. With three sure trump tricks it may be tempting to double, but think what will happen if they run to another suit. Might not your partner double expecting you to have some help in the defence? If so he will be sorely disappointed. The only suit you like is clubs so keep quiet and don't risk scaring them away (**9**).

THE OPPONENTS MAKE A TAKEOUT DOUBLE

If your partner opens one of a suit and the next hand doubles, there is no point in thinking that you like partner's suit and have a reasonable hand so the best option is simply to pass because he will make it easily. The double is for takeout and somebody is going to bid.

Mostly, the rules are much the same as if your opponents had not doubled, i.e. a new suit at the one level shows 6+ HCP, and at the two level 9+ HCP. There are a number of differences, however.

Firstly, suppose the bidding begins 1◊ – Double –? How should you bid these hands (**1,2**)?

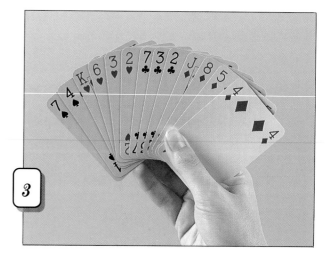

When somebody makes a takeout double they show interest in all the suits except the one opened. Probably there is little point in bidding a weak four-card suit as in (**1**); it is better to forget about the hearts and bid 1NT to show the all-round nature of your hand. Hand (**2**), however, has all its strength in the four-card suit and even playing in a 4-3 fit will be tolerable, so bid 1♡, if only to make sure partner leads one if you end up defending.

Secondly, if you have support for partner's suit you should strain to raise him as high as you can. The reason is simple; if one side has a fit then the other side is bound to have a fit also. The higher you can raise the bidding, the harder it may be for them to find their best suit. So whenever you have a close decision how high to raise, take the aggressive course.

After 1♡ – Double – ?, how should you bid these hands (**3, 4**)?

Raise to 2♡ with (**3**) and 3♡ with (**4**), even though without the double you might have passed and bid 2♡ respectively. Don't worry if partner is left to play and goes down. That just makes it more certain that your opponents had the strength to make a contract themselves if they had bid one, so you will probably still show a profit.

You also have one new option, you can redouble. If that ended the auction, it would mean that the scores would be multiplied by four instead of two for a doubled contract, but of course the double was for takeout, so someone else will normally bid.

A redouble does not just mean you expect partner's contract to make – there would be little point in that as he will not be allowed to play it. It tells partner that you have 9+ HCP so your side has the balance of strength and invites him to cooperate in trying to penalize the opposition.

After 1♡ – Double – Redouble – 1♠ – ?, how should you bid these hands (**5-8**)?

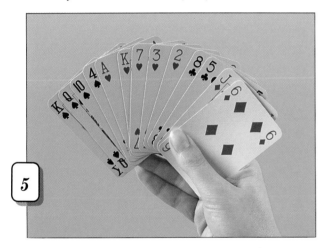

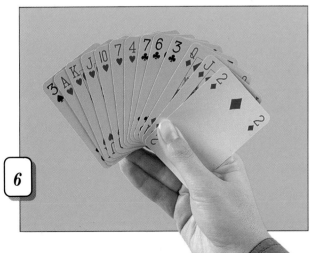

(**5**) should double. You have excellent spades and with your side having the balance of strength can hope for a useful penalty.

(**6**) Bid 2♡. You only opened because of the heart suit and have no interest in defending. Show your long suit and minimum opening by bidding 2♡.

(**7**) Bid 2◊. Again, you opened only because of your distribution. Bid 2◊ to show your weakish two-suiter.

(**8**) Pass. If you have the balance of the strength, it cannot make sense to let your opponents play undoubled at the one level. The rule is that they cannot do so; either you must double them or bid something yourselves. Here, you would be happy to defend but cannot double without trumps. Not to worry; your pass forces partner to speak. If he has spades he will double and you can pass happily; if not, he will bid something else and you can bid 4♡ or 3NT as seems appropriate.

Be sure that you understand this idea before you move on because, while quite logical, the idea of a pass being forcing may seem quite strange at first.

DEFENSIVE SIGNALLING

Ýou lead an honour card and it holds the trick. How do you know whether to continue the suit or to switch to another one?

The answer is that you need partner to signal whether he likes the suit. This does not mean that he smiles and nods if he approves of the lead and frowns if he does not like it. That, to put it bluntly, would be cheating. What is perfectly legal is to signal with the actual cards you play. The traditional way to do this is to play an unnecessarily high card to encourage partner to continue his suit, the smallest card possible to discourage, i.e. suggest a switch to a different suit. This is known as an **attitude signal**.

The obvious time to encourage partner to continue to lead the same suit is when you have strength in it. For example, suppose partner leads an ace and dummy holds three small cards. Normally, if partner leads an ace she will also hold the king. Holding Q82 you would play the eight to encourage a continuation, with 832 you would play the two to discourage. Let's look at this from the opening leader's point of view (**1**).

You lead the king and it holds the trick. Now, does your partner hold either the jack or ace in which case you want to lead the seven next, or has declarer ducked from AJx when you need the next lead of the suit to come from partner?

Partner knows you hold king-queen. If she holds either the ace or the jack she will play her highest spot card, e.g. eight from A-8-2 or J-8-2; with no honour she will pay small, two from 8-3-2.

In this example (**2**) you lead your ace (**3**) and can continue if partner encourages, showing the queen, but must switch if she plays a small card to deny the queen.

In a suit contract you may encourage because you want a ruff. When partner leads the ace in this example (**4**), you signal with the nine (**5**), knowing that you can trump the third round.

When declarer leads a suit, it is not normal to encourage and discourage. Instead, if you think it will help partner you can give a **count signal**, showing partner how many cards you hold in the suit led.

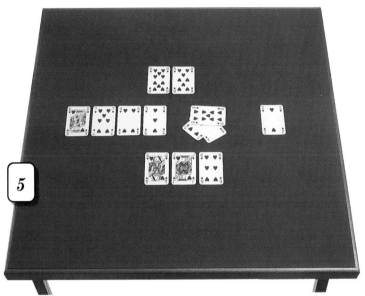

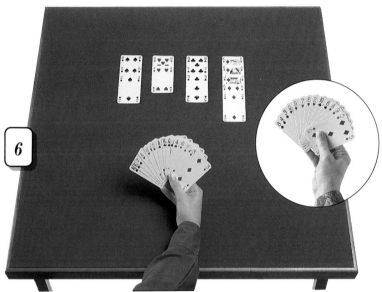

If declarer holds the hand shown (**6**), you must duck two rounds of diamonds. Now careful defence holds her to eight tricks – two spades, one heart, two diamonds and three clubs.

If declarer holds the hand shown in (**7**), ducking the second diamond gives declarer her ninth trick – two spades, one heart, two diamonds and four clubs. Partner's count signal solves your problem. If declarer has hand (**6**), partner has two diamonds and will play high-low, so you know to duck twice.

If declarer has hand (**7**), partner has three diamonds and will play low-high, so you know to win the second round. All you need to do is to count to 13.

With an odd number – one, three or five – you play your smallest card. With an even number – two, four or six – you play high then low, as if you were encouraging. So, holding:

(i) 8-3-2 Play the two, bottom of an odd number.
(ii) 9-4 Play the nine, top of a doubleton.
(iii) 9-6-3-2 Play the six, clearer than the three, intending to play the two next and show an even number. This high-low signal is sometimes known as a **peter** or **echo**.

Now look at this example (**6**). South opens 2NT and is raised to game. Partner leads ♠Q and declarer wins the king and leads ◇10 then a second diamond to dummy's king. Should you win this or duck, making sure of cutting declarer off from the rest of dummy's diamonds?

DEFENSIVE PLANNING

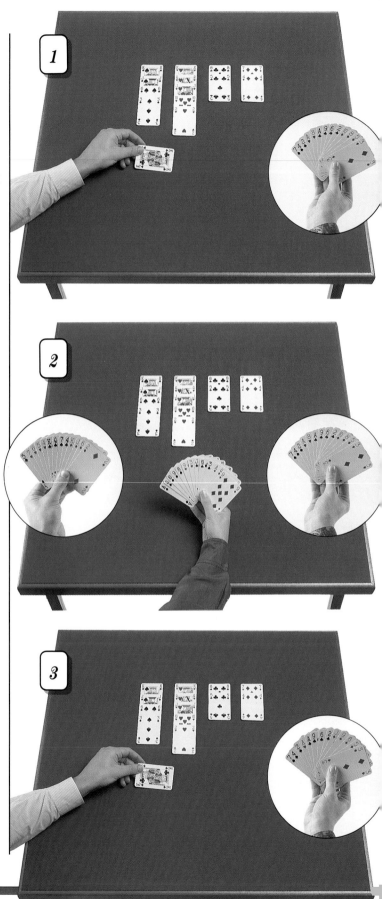

We saw earlier how important it was for declarer to have a plan of campaign. It is just as vital that the defenders try to make a plan rather than just take the tricks that are staring them in the face, then look around for more.

Declarer can see all her side's combined assets. It is true that the defenders are not so fortunately placed, but they do have a lot of information at their disposal.

Firstly, there is the bidding. Both the bids made and, just as importantly, those not made help to give a picture of declarer's hand and partner's. Secondly, the opening lead tells you a lot about partner's holding, and thirdly your defensive signalling allows you to help each other and to build up a mental picture of the complete deal.

Perhaps the most important single piece of information available to you is the contract. That tells you how many tricks you are aiming for. If the contract is 4♡, for example, declarer's target is ten tricks, therefore yours is four – very simple. Your plan should always bear this in mind.

Consider these examples (**1-6**). In each case the auction is:

South	North
1♠	2♡
2♠	4♠
Pass	

and partner leads the ♣K (**1**).

You know partner has ♣KQ and you like the suit so you encourage with the nine. Partner plays ♣4 to your ace. Now what?

The ♡A is your third trick but once it is gone declarer can discard all her losers on the established hearts. Partner may have ♠A, otherwise you need a diamond trick. Switch to a diamond now. If partner has ◇K you establish your fourth trick while you still control the hearts. The full deal is shown in picture (**2**).

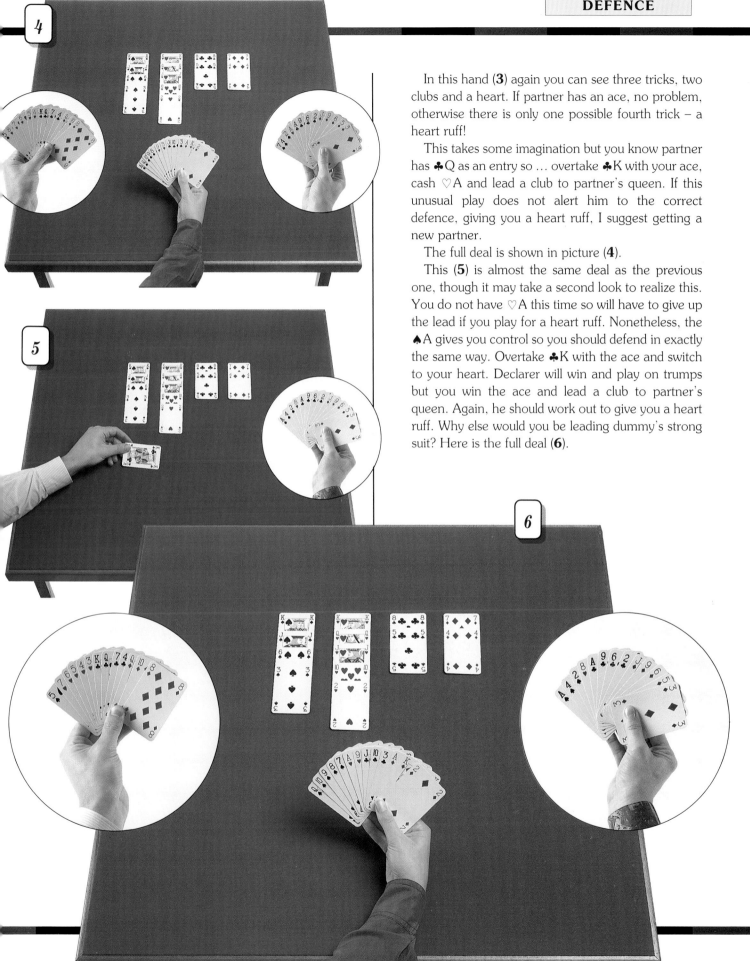

In this hand (**3**) again you can see three tricks, two clubs and a heart. If partner has an ace, no problem, otherwise there is only one possible fourth trick – a heart ruff!

This takes some imagination but you know partner has ♣Q as an entry so ... overtake ♣K with your ace, cash ♡A and lead a club to partner's queen. If this unusual play does not alert him to the correct defence, giving you a heart ruff, I suggest getting a new partner.

The full deal is shown in picture (**4**).

This (**5**) is almost the same deal as the previous one, though it may take a second look to realize this. You do not have ♡A this time so will have to give up the lead if you play for a heart ruff. Nonetheless, the ♠A gives you control so you should defend in exactly the same way. Overtake ♣K with the ace and switch to your heart. Declarer will win and play on trumps but you win the ace and lead a club to partner's queen. Again, he should work out to give you a heart ruff. Why else would you be leading dummy's strong suit? Here is the full deal (**6**).

DUCKING IN DEFENCE

I would not wish to give the impression that you should never take an ace or king at the first opportunity. There are many occasions when it is right to do so. Just as for declarer, however, there are also many occasions when it is right for a defender to let his opponent win a trick which he could have won himself.

One reason to do this is in an attempt to disrupt declarer's communications. We saw an example of this in the section on defensive signalling where it was important to use count signals to decide when to take an ace when dummy had no outside entry.

This deal (**1**) illustrates the same theme. West leads ♠Q against South's 3NT contract. Declarer wins the king, and finesses ♣Q. If East wins the king declarer has no further worries, taking at least four clubs, two dia-

monds, two spades and a heart. Nine tricks – the contract is made.

Now play the hand through again with East ducking the first club. That restricts declarer to at most two club tricks and twist and turn as she might, she cannot make more than eight tricks in total. One more thing; if you are going to duck, do it smoothly. Why tell declarer what is going on?

A second rèason to duck a trick is to keep your own communications open. Consider this example (**2**). South plays in 3NT and West leads ♡5. Declarer plays low from dummy so East wins the queen and returns the nine (when you return partner's lead it is correct to lead your original fourth highest with four or more but the higher of two remaining cards).

If West wins the second heart with the ace, he can play a third round to clear the suit but then has no entry to his winners. If, on the other hand, he ducks the second heart, East can win the ace when declarer plays on clubs and has a heart left to lead to West's ace. Now West is on lead and is the only one with hearts so can cash his two winners for one down. Set

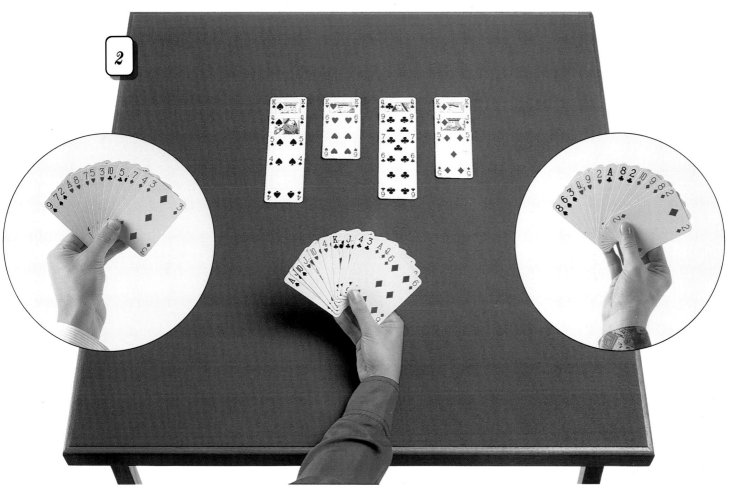

up the deal with a pack of cards and play it through both ways to see the difference.

A third reason to duck a trick is simply to leave declarer in the dark about the position of the missing high cards. Perhaps this will make a subsequent guess, either in the same suit or elsewhere, more difficult. Take this example (**3**).

South plays in 6NT on the lead of the ♡10. She wins with the jack and leads a spade to the king. Suppose East wins the ace or, even worse, thinks for a while then ducks. In either case declarer's next spade play will be low to the ten, hoping to find West with the jack. Her hopes will be realized and she will make her slam. Now see what happens if East ducks the first spade smoothly. Declarer has no clue as to the spade position. When she leads up towards the remaining queen-ten she will have a horrible 50-50 guess. Remember, she does not have the benefit of seeing all four hands.

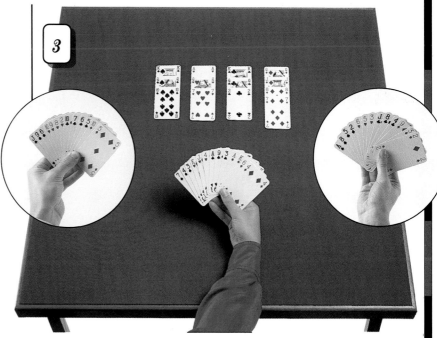

COUNTING IN DEFENCE

Counting is hard work at first but if you persevere it gets easier and it is well worth the effort. Counting can help you in your defensive planning in many different ways.

Counting points while remembering the bidding will sometimes tell you whether it is declarer or partner who has a missing high card.

Counting cards can allow you to build up a precise picture of the distribution of the unseen hands. This could, for example, help you to know which of two winners to keep for the final trick.

Counting declarer's tricks may tell you whether a patient passive defence has a chance of success or whether your only chance is to try something risky and gamble on partner having what you need. To try to defend without counting is like hoping to appreciate a rose when you have no sense of smell or are colourblind.

On this hand (**1**) South opens 1NT (15-17) and is raised to 3NT. Partner leads ♣6 to your queen and declarer's king. Declarer plays a spade to the queen and leads ♡J from dummy. Do you take the ace or duck?

If you assume that partner has led his fourth highest club, then the rule of eleven tells you that declarer has no more cards higher than the six (11-6 = 5 and you can see four cards higher than the six between your hand and dummy plus declarer's king). So partner has the ace and jack of clubs.

Try counting points. Dummy has 13, you have seven and partner has five – so declarer must have all the rest. This is the full deal (**2**).

If you duck the heart you allow declarer to steal her ninth trick. Then she will run for home. Rise with the ace of hearts and lead clubs, hoping partner has five to beat the contract.

In this case (**3**) the bidding goes:

South	North
1♡	4♡
6♡	Pass

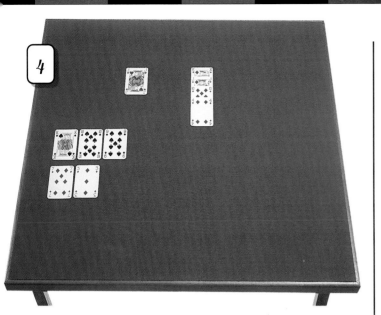

You lead the ♣Q and declarer wins the king, cashes ♠A and plays three rounds of trumps ending in the dummy. Partner follows to one heart then discards a club and a spade. Declarer ruffs dummy's ♠J, then plays ace and another club, partner following both times. You are on lead and can see (**4**).

You know declarer is void in spades, so it looks natural to lead a diamond rather than give her a ruff and discard. Let's count first though. Declarer is known to have started with five hearts, one spade and three clubs and therefore must have four diamonds. In that case a ruff and discard cannot help her while a diamond would save her the crucial guess. Lead a spade and leave declarer to find the ◇Q herself. This is how the whole deal looked (**5**).

Here is another example (**6**). The bidding goes:

South	West	North	East
–	–	1♣	1♠
1NT	Pass	3NT	All Pass

Partner leads ♠8 and dummy plays low. How do you defend?

It looks obvious to play low. The eight will force out declarer's king and you will be able to cash the rest of the suit as soon as you gain the lead. But wait a minute. There are six club tricks in dummy. If declarer wins ♠K she has at least nine tricks; ten if she has ◇K and nine, courtesy of the winning diamond finesse, if she does not have ◇K. Your only chance to beat 3NT is to rise with ♠A and switch to ace and queen of hearts, hoping the full deal is as seen in (**7**).

PART THREE

MORE ADVANCED PLAY

STRONG OPENINGS – TWO NO TRUMPS

Some hands are just too powerful to be opened at the one level. The problem is that partner might pass when you have enough between you to want to play in game. Opening bids at the two level are used to show these very powerful hands. There are three different kinds of two level opening, with quite different meanings. We will look at each in turn starting with 2NT.

THE 2NT OPENING

An opening bid of 2NT shows a balanced hand with 20-22 HCP. Just like a 1NT opening it gives a fairly accurate picture of opener's hand immediately, so responder will often be in a position to choose the final contract. Though a 2NT opening does not compel partner to bid, he will obviously do so far more often than not when facing what is known to be a very strong hand. The scheme of responses is as follows:

Pass. Any hand which is too weak to play in game whatever the distribution. There is no weakness take-out into a long suit as we saw over the 1NT opening, you just pass and pray.

To go on to game, responder needs around five points; or four points and a five-card suit; or three points and a six-card suit; otherwise he passes. These hands should both pass a 2NT opening (**1, 2**).

3NT. This shows a flattish 5-10 points, though a long minor suit is allowed as 3NT may prove easier than five of the minor. Opener should always pass a raise to 3NT. These are typical 3NT hands (**3, 4**).

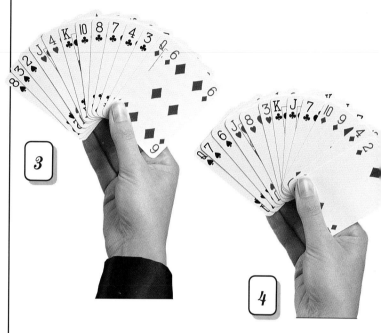

4NT. This shows a balanced 11-12 points and invites slam. Partner is expected to pass with a minimum but raise to 6NT with a maximum hand for his 2NT opening. These (**5, 6**) are typical 4NT bids.

3♢/♡/♠. These are all natural bids, promising at least a five-card suit and forcing to at least game.

With (**7**) all you want is to get partner to choose between 4♡ and 3NT. You respond 3♡ and whichever he chooses you will pass. Normally he will bid 3NT with a doubleton in your suit or perhaps three small, but support you with honour to three or better. With (**8**) you respond 3♠ but intend to look for a slam. If partner raises to 4♠ you will bid 5♠ or 6♠ according to how optimistic you are feeling (but see the section on slam bidding later in the book), while you will raise 3NT to 4NT to invite 6NT.

4♡/♠: These bids show at least a six-card suit and are strictly to play. Partner is not being invited to bid again. Examples are shown here (**9, 10**).

3♣: This is Stayman and works just like 1NT – 2♣. It guarantees at least one four-card major plus game values. Hands (**11, 12**) are examples.

Opener responds as follows:

2NT – 3♣ – 3♢ = No four-card major, it has nothing to do with diamonds.

    – 3♡ = Four hearts, may or may not have four spades.

    – 3♠ = Four spades, denies four hearts.

STRONG OPENINGS – TWO OF A SUIT

Opening bids of 2◇/♡/♠ show powerful hands with at least a strong five-card suit. When deciding whether to open one of a suit or two, you look more at playing tricks than at HCP, needing eight or more to qualify for a two opening. Assuming partner has two or three small cards in the suit, this is how you might assess the playing tricks available.

- AKQJ6 = Five
- AKJ943 = Five
- KQJ108 = Four
- AK762 = Three and a half
- A = One
- AQ = One and a half
- KQ7 = One and a half

The reason for opening two of a suit is fear of missing a game if you open one and partner passes. After a two of a suit opening partner must bid, even with nothing, to give you a second chance. This will be especially valuable if you have a second suit to show. Hands (**1** and **2**) would be suitable for a 2♡ opening bid. The responses are as follows:

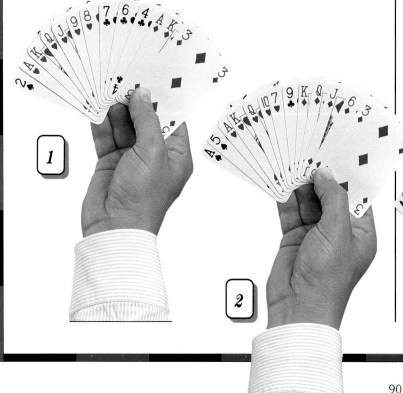

2NT. This is the weakness response. It is bid on all bad hands whatever their shape and has nothing whatsoever to do with a wish to play in No Trumps. It is bid on all hands with 0-6 HCP and also some slightly stronger hands which do not fit in anywhere else. Opposite 2♡, bid 2NT with these hands (**3, 4**).

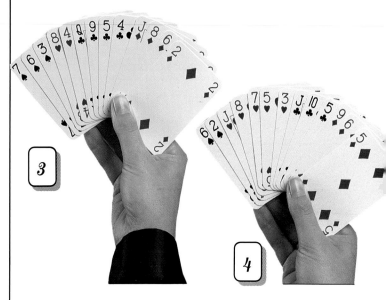

With (**4**) you bid 2NT despite your heart support. Warn partner of your weakness first. He is obliged to bid again as you have not said you want to play in 2NT so you can support hearts next time.

All other responses are positives, showing 7+ HCP and forcing to at least game.

The Single Raise: 2♡–3♡

This shows heart support and a hand with some potential for slam, usually (though not always) with at least one ace. Because opener guaranteed a long strong suit, you can raise with as little as three small or queen doubleton trump. Here are examples (**5, 6**).

The Double Raise: 2♡–4♡

This also shows positive values and heart support but denies an ace. The difference is to help opener decide whether to look for a slam. It is a way of warning him that, despite the trump fit and great combined strength, slam is unlikely unless he has many aces and kings. These are hands that would qualify for a double raise (**7, 8**).

3NT. Shows a balanced hand of around 10-12 HCP but no genuine support for partner's suit. Hand (**9**) is a typical example.

A NEW SUIT: 2♡–2♠/3♣/♢

This promises a good five-card suit. Since opener has shown a good long suit of his own, he will not be interested in your suit unless it also is a good one. The response in a new suit, like all positives, is forcing to game and subsequent bidding is on normal lines, each player bidding his suits until a fit is found. Both these hands would entitle you to bid a new suit (**10, 11**).

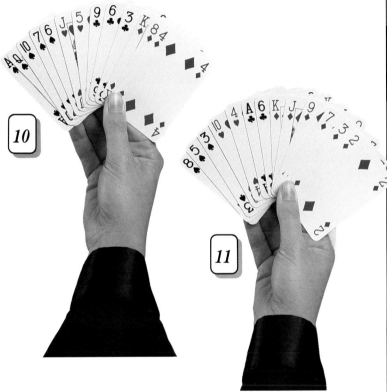

SECOND ROUND BIDDING

After the negative 2NT response, opener rebids naturally. Only if he jumps is the auction forcing to game.

After 2♡ – 2NT – 3♡; how would you, responder, bid on these hands?

(i)	♠	J642	(ii)	♠	10642
	♡	Q6		♡	Q6
	♢	J853		♢	A853
	♣	J43		♣	743

(i) should pass as you have only one likely trick to add to partner's eight. (ii), with two good cards, should raise to game.

STRONG OPENINGS – TWO CLUBS

You will have noticed that 2♣ was not included in the previous discussion of two of a suit opening bids. This is because it is used in a slightly different way. A 2♣ opening shows a very powerful hand, even stronger than 2◇/♡/♠, but it has nothing at all to do with clubs. With the exception of one sequence, it is completely forcing to game even if responder has nothing.

TYPICAL 2♣ OPENERS

These two hands (**1, 2**) are typical of what you need to open 2♣. Both are real powerhouses

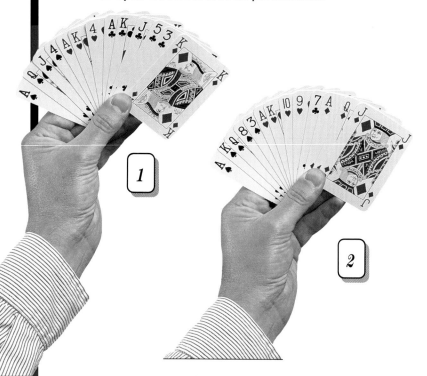

RESPONDING TO 2♣

2◇: The negative response covering all hands with 0-6 HCP and some hands with seven or eight points which do not conveniently fit into any other response. It says nothing about diamonds. All other responses are positives, showing 7+ HCP.

2♡/♠: Natural, 7+ HCP, a good four- or reasonable five-card suit.

2NT: A flattish 7-9 HCP. It may include a five-card suit which is far too weak to bid. Both these examples are best started with 2NT (**3, 4**).

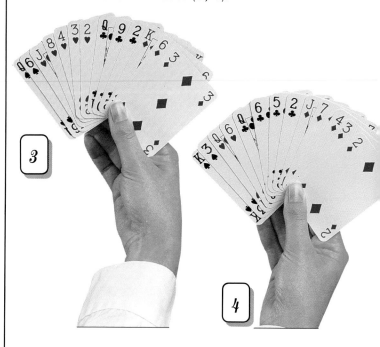

3♣/◇: 7+ HCP and a reasonable five-card suit. Where example (**4**) above is not worth a 3◇ response, example (**5**) would be.

3♡/♠: A rare response showing a solid six-card or longer suit, AKQJxx or better.

3NT: 10-12 HCP and a balanced hand.

Though the shapes and strengths are identical, the initial responses should not be. With its scattered values, (**6A**) is a classic 3NT response. (**6B**) should respond 2♡, stressing the excellent four-card suit.

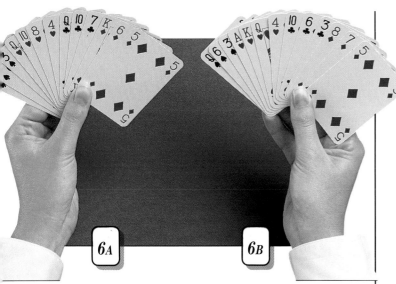

second suit. Note that West passes 4♡ despite his huge hand. Having opened 2♣ he has already shown a very strong hand so has little to spare. If slam was possible, East should have bid more than just 4♡.

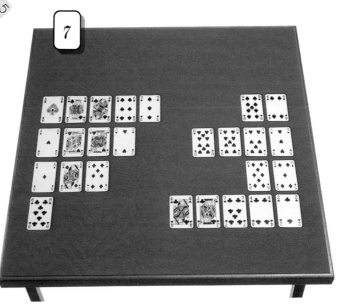

West	East
2♣	2♢
3♣	3♢
3♠	3NT
Pass	

Again, in this example (**8**), the start is the strong 2♣ and 2♢ is the negative. Remembering that neither clubs nor diamonds were bid naturally, the players now bid their long suits. Over 3♢, West bids his second suit and, with no support for either clubs or spades and only five diamonds, East can only try 3NT, which West passes as he has already described his hand.

SUBSEQUENT BIDDING

2♣ – 2♢ – 2NT shows a balanced hand with 23-24 HCP, just too strong for a 2NT opening bid. It is the only sequence which can be passed short of game. With nothing, responder may pass 2NT, but, facing such a strong hand, as little as one king or a queen and a jack should persuade him to raise to game.

All other responses have the same meaning as opposite a 2NT opening, i.e. 3♣ is Stayman and 3♢/♡/♠ is forcing with at least a five-card suit.

All other sequences are game forcing, whether the initial response was 2♢ or not. This allows opener, with a very strong hand, to explore properly for a trump fit without having to worry about being left stranded in some obscure partscore.

Bidding follows standard rules, i.e. each player bids his suits in order, longest first until a fit is found. Other rules such as bidding the higher of two five-card suits first but the lower of two four-card suits are also followed. Remember that the 2♣ opening and 2♢ response were artificial.

West	East
2♣	2♢
2♠	3♣
3♡	4♡
Pass	

In this example (**7**), West opens 2♣ because he has a very powerful hand and East makes the negative response. Now each player in turn bids his longest suit. West tries again and East is happy to raise the

OPENING BIDS AT THE THREE LEVEL

An opening bid of three of a suit is known as a **pre-empt** or a **pre-emptive opening bid**. It shows a long strong suit but very few high cards, normally less than would be required to open at the one level. A typical 3♡ opening might be (**1**).

The idea is firstly to warn partner that your hand is of a special type, useful only if your suit is trumps, and secondly to make life very difficult for your opponents. Because you have very little defensive strength, they might well have a good contract on their way if they can find it. You can imagine, given how difficult bidding can sometimes seem even when you are left to yourselves, how awkward it can be if somebody opens at the three level before you have even started.

Though you have little defensive strength, your long suit means you should be able to make quite a few tricks if you are left to play in your pre-empt so will not come to too much harm. Often, if you go down it means your opponents had enough strength to make a contract had they bid one, so you still make a profit from your bid.

The requirements for a pre-emptive opening are a reasonable seven-card suit and not too much defensive strength outside. You need to be a little stronger when vulnerable than when non-vulnerable, simply because each undertrick costs you more when you go down. You should beware of having second suits which could make good trump suits if partner also has four or more of them. The message when you open at the three level is that your hand is only any use if your suit is trumps.

Hand (**2**) is worth a 3♡ opening when non-vulnerable, but is a trick too weak if vulnerable when you could easily concede a penalty bigger than anything the opposition could make themselves.

(**3**) is a 3♡ opening whether vulnerable or not. The suit is excellent and you have a possible trick outside.

(**4**) is a 3♡ opening because the side suit is a weak one. You have no defence and partner would need very good diamonds for them to make a good trump suit.

(**5**) should probably pass. The diamonds not only offer an alternative trump suit but also good defensive values, making it hard for partner to judge after a 3♡ opening. Pass, intending to bid next time.

(**9**) Bid 4♡. 3NT may look obvious, but you will need several heart tricks to make game and how will you ever get to her hand to cash them? You need hearts as trumps so you can ruff something to get at your winners.

(**6**) should pass. The suit is too weak for a pre-empt and you have too much outside defensive strength.

(**7**) is right on point count but has too much playing strength for a 3♡ opening. Open 4♡, which is just a bigger version of a 3♡ opening, showing very long hearts but still not many high cards.

RESPONDING TO A PRE-EMPT

The three level opening is very precise. Often, responder is in a very good position to choose the final contract. Unless he has both a very good suit of his own and considerable strength, the choices will usually be pass, 3NT, and a raise of opener's suit.

Remember the sort of hand partner has promised. Simply counting points will not do as all your queens and jacks may be useless in her short suits. Instead, count likely tricks – aces, kings, trump honours and ruffs. Assume opener has about six tricks non-vulnerable and seven vulnerable. Add your quick tricks to hers and either pass or bid game.

PARTNER OPENS 3♡

If your partner makes a pre-emptive opening bid of 3♡, what should you bid with these hands (**8-11**)?

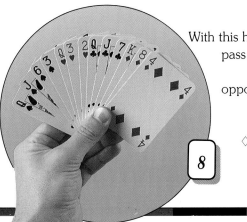

With this hand (**8**) you should pass. Your honours will mostly be useless opposite her shortages. Imagine she has ♠105 ♡AKJ7654 ◇J3 ♣84 or similar to see why.

(**10**) Bid 3NT. This is the reverse of hand (**9**). If partner has ♡KQ107532 and nothing else, you can count nine tricks and you have every suit stopped. But can you be sure of ten tricks if you bid 4♡?

With this hand (**11**), bid 4♡. You know you cannot really make anything but if you have eleven hearts between you and few high cards then the opposition can make a lot. Make it harder for them by continuing the pre-empt.

One final rule: having pre-empted you only bid again if partner forces you to do so by responding in a new suit. Otherwise, trust her decisions. She knows your hand quite well while you have no idea about hers.

DEFENDING AGAINST PRE-EMPTS

The whole point of pre-empting is to make life difficult for the opposition and to make them guess. Inevitably, when your opponent opens at the three level or higher, you will not guess right all the time – nobody does. The best you can do is to follow a sensible set of rules and keep your fingers crossed.

The actual meaning of a bid over an opposing pre-empt is much the same as that over a one level opening. In other words, an overcall shows a good long suit, a No Trump bid shows a stopper in the opener's suit and a strong fairly balanced hand, and a double is for takeout. That is not to say that every hand which would bid over a one level opening should automatically bid over a three level opening. You have to balance the risk of missing a good contract against the danger of bidding at such a high level, so need a little extra strength.

An overcall should show a six-card or very strong five-card suit which would have opened the bidding had it had the chance. 12 HCP will do with a six-card suit, about 14 HCP with only five. With a very strong hand with a six-card or longer suit, say 19 or 20 HCP upwards, take the pressure off partner by jumping all the way to game yourself. Over a 3♣ opening, how would you bid these hands (**1-3**)?

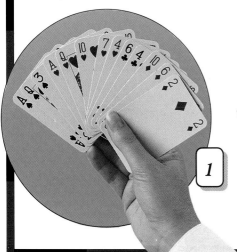

(**1**) Though you would have bid 1♡ over 1♣, this hand is not quite strong enough to bid 3♡ over 3♣. It is best to pass.

(**2**) Now you have a sound 3♡ overcall. It is as much the extra heart as the extra couple of points that make this hand more suitable than (**1**).

(**3**) Jump to 4♡. You cannot guarantee to make this, but need so little help from partner that you cannot expect him to raise 3♡ to game often enough.

THE 3NT OVERCALL

A 3NT overcall requires around 17+ HCP but can be tried on slightly less if you hold a long suit as a potential source of tricks. The same bid may be made on quite a lot more than that, after all partner may be very weak and while you sometimes have to gamble, it is comforting occasionally to have all the strength you need yourself. One essential is that you must have opener's suit stopped.

All these hands should bid 3NT over a 3♣ opening.

(i)   ♠ Q107   (ii) ♠ AQ10   (iii) ♠ J54
    ♡ A86   ♡ AJ6   ♡ A8
    ◇ AQJ2   ◇ AQJ2   ◇ KQJ963
    ♣ KJ4   ♣ AQ4   ♣ AQ

You might instinctively bid 3◇ on (iii). This would not be a bad bid, but the large bonus for bidding and making a game is well worth having and, with clubs well held and diamonds a source of several tricks, you do not need much help from partner to make 3NT.

A double is for takeout and promises sound opening bid values and usually support for the other three suits. As usual, the more ideal your shape, the less high cards are needed. These would all be minimum doubles of a 3♣ opening.

(iv) ♠ QJ108 (v) ♠ AJ108 (vi) ♠ AJ8
  ♡ K1086   ♡ K1086   ♡ AJ108
  ◇ AQ54   ◇ AQ5   ◇ AQ5
  ♣ 6   ♣ 74   ♣ 874

When partner bids over a pre-empt, whether with an overcall or a takeout double, you have to allow for the fact that he was under pressure. The basic rule is to discount the first 7 or 8 HCP in your hand and only make a positive bid if you have even more. For partner to risk bidding at all at such a high level he had to assume you had some strength.

QUIZ HANDS

After 3♣ – 3♠ – Pass – ?, what would you bid on these hands (**4-6**)?

(**4**) Pass. Partner already assumed you held this much.

(**5**) With ten good points, raise to 4♠.

(**6**) Only two spades but 10 HCP and an excellent club stopper; try 3NT.

After 3♣ – Double – Pass – ?, what would you bid here (**7-9**)?

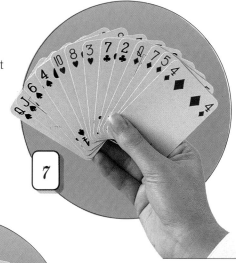

(**7**) Bid 3♠. With a choice, bid the major as it scores more and partner tends to be more careful always to have support for unbid majors.

(**8**) Jump to 4♡, just as you would have jumped to 2♡ over a double of 1♣.

(**9**) Pass. You cannot guarantee to make a game, but with two probable trump tricks and an ace-king can hope for a juicy penalty out of three clubs doubled.

The most important thing when somebody pre-empts against you is just to have the right attitude of mind. Accept that you are in an awkward position and try always to get a sensible result rather than always strive for perfection and risk something ridiculous happening.

DECLARER PLAY – TRUMP CONTRACTS

Possession of a trump suit can help declarer in many ways. One advantage it gives her is the ability to ruff her opponents' winners. This is something of a two-edged sword, of course, because it also means that the defenders can sometimes ruff her winners. An important question then is whether or not to draw trumps?

There is no simple answer to this question. Sometimes it is right to draw trumps immediately, sometimes to delay drawing them at all. Take these two extreme examples: (**1**, **2**).

Again (**2**) South is in 4♠ on a low diamond lead, East playing the queen. Should she again draw trumps? Most assuredly not. She has three heart losers so cannot afford to lose even one diamond trick. If she draws trumps it will take a minimum of two rounds. That will leave at most two trumps in dummy to take care of four small diamonds. Even a single round of trumps could prove fatal. This hand should be played on a complete cross-ruff. Win the ace of diamonds and alternately ruff diamonds and clubs until you have run out of trumps. You make all nine trumps separately plus the ◇A, leaving the defence to take the last three tricks.

In real-life, the issue may not always be so clearcut. Take this hand (**3**).

South plays 4♡ on the lead of the ♠Q. She plays low from dummy as West will not have underled the ace and ruffs in hand. If she draws trumps then knocks out the ♣A, the defence can take three diamonds and a club for one down. She needs the control given by dummy's trumps and doubleton diamond.

Declarer should knock out the ♣A before drawing trumps. True, this runs the risk of conceding a club ruff, but if she is lucky they will be 2-2. She can draw trumps as soon as she regains the lead and cash her club winners.

In (**1**) South plays in 4♠ on the lead of a low diamond. This is a case where it is clearly right to draw all the outstanding trumps as quickly as possible. By knocking out the missing aces declarer can make all the tricks she needs by sheer force of high cards. She has no need of either the extra tricks or control sometimes provided by a trump suit. On the contrary, the only way she will fail is if some of her high card winners are trumped by the defence.

In this hand (**4**) South plays 2♡ on the lead of the ♠2. If both red suits broke 3-3, declarer could win, play three rounds of trumps and, after ruffing the next spade, duck a diamond to establish her eighth trick. The surer way to success is, however, to take the opening lead at face value. If the two is fourth highest then spades are 4-4 between East and West. In that case declarer does not need to rely on an even break in any other suit but uses her three dummy entries to ruff spades, making all her low trumps in hand plus ♡AK, ◇AK and ♠A – eight tricks.

PLAY SUMMARY BOX												
TRICK												
1	**2**	**3**	**4**	**5**	**6**	**7**	**8**	**9**	**10**	**11**	**12**	**13**
W	N	S	N	S	N	S	S					
♠2	♠4	◇4	♠6	◇5	♠J	♡A	♡K					
N	E	W	E	W	E	W	W					
♠A	♠7	◇3	♠9	◇J	♠Q	♡4	♡7					
E	S	N	S	N	S	N	N					
♠5	♡3	◇A	♡8	◇K	♡9	♡5	♡6					
S	W	E	W	E	W	E	E					
♠3	♠8	◇6	♠10	◇7	♠K	♡2	♡J					

CARD READING

The bidding can offer valuable clues regarding the position of missing high cards and the distribution of the defenders' hands. It is reasonable to assume that a player who passes up an opportunity to make a particular bid does not have a hand which was suitable for that bid. Having made that assumption, you can plan your play accordingly.

These are a few of the soundest inferences you can draw from your opponents' bidding. There are many others which you will pick up as you gain experience.
• A player who does not open the bidding when he had the chance to do so will not have a good 12 HCP or more.
• A player who passes his partner's opening bid of one of a suit will have less than 6 HCP.
• A hand which does not open 1NT will not be both balanced *and* the right strength for the bid.
• A player who does not overcall at the one level will not have both a good five-card suit *and* an outside ace or king.

Keeping a count of the defenders' shape and high cards will often help you to "guess" correctly.

West	North	East	South
Pass	Pass	Pass	1♠
Pass	2♠	Pass	4♠
All Pass			

In this hand (**1**) West leads the ace, king and queen of hearts then switches to the ◇J. Having won the ◇A, you should play a spade to the ace. Dropping the singleton king is substantially against the odds, but you know it is your only chance. Why? Because West passed as dealer and has already shown up with ten points; he *cannot* have the ♠K also so the finesse is doomed. This is how the whole hand looks (**2**).

West	North	East	South
1◇	Pass	Pass	1NT
Pass	3NT	All Pass	

This one (**3**) is more difficult. West leads the king, queen and jack of clubs, East following each time, and you win the third round. You play on spades and West wins the ace and cashes the thirteenth club. You throw a heart from dummy, as does East and a diamond from hand. West exits with a heart and you finesse the queen successfully. You cash the ♡A but the king does not drop, then the rest of the spades, West throwing a diamond on the fourth spade and East a heart. Who has the ◇Q?

West is known to have started with precisely 3-3-3-4 shape from the play to date. All you need to know is what strength of No Trump opening your opponents play. With a balanced hand, West would have opened 1NT if he had the right strength. So far he has shown up with 13 HCP – ♠A, ♡K, ♣KQJ. If he is playing a strong No Trump (15-17) he must have ◇Q, if playing a weak No Trump (12-14) he cannot have it. You should finesse accordingly.

	PLAY SUMMARY BOX											
TRICK												
1	**2**	**3**	**4**	**5**	**6**	**7**	**8**	**9**	**10**	**11**	**12**	**13**
W	W	W	S	W	W	N	N	N	N			
♣K	♣Q	♣J	♠K	♣10	♡2	♡A	♠Q	♠J	♠9			
N	N	N	W	N	N	E	E	E	E			
♣3	♣6	♣9	♠A	♡3	♡Q	♡9	♠4	♠5	♡10			
E	E	E	N	E	E	S	S	S	S			
♣4	♣5	♣8	♠3	♡4	♡6	-♡7	♠6	♠10	♡J			
S	S	S	E	S	S	W	W	W	W			
♣2	♣7	♣A	♠2	◇4	♡5	♡8	♠7	♠8	◇2			

CLUES FROM THE OPENING LEAD

Most defenders find that solid honour sequences are very attractive opening leads. Generally, a player who leads a small card is unlikely to hold such a sequence. Take a look at hand (**4**).

West	North	East	South
1◇	Pass	Pass	2♠
Pass	4♠	All Pass	

West leads ♡3 against 4♠. What information does this give you? Surely West does not have the ace and king of diamonds or he would have led one. So East has at least the ◇K and cannot therefore have another king as she failed to respond to 1◇.

This tells you that the spade finesse is sure to fail, so you should just lay down the ace, and that the club finesse is sure to succeed, allowing you to take it, then discard a diamond on the ace. Here is the complete hand (**5**).

SUIT COMBINATIONS

While one should always try to play the whole hand correctly rather than play suits in isolation, it is still a good idea to know the best way to tackle common suit combinations.

The play can often revolve around the hunt for a missing queen. Take this situation (**1**). Missing four cards including the queen, the best chance is to cash the ace and king.

Missing five cards (**2**) you should guess to cash the ace or king then finesse. To see why, imagine the missing cards are divided 3-2. The queen is more likely to be in the three than in the two, isn't it, by odds of 3 to 2. So the finesse is more likely to work than playing for the drop.

In this case (**3**) take a first round finesse and, if it succeeds, go back to dummy to finesse again. Cashing the ace first gains when West has the bare queen but loses when he has any of the four small singletons as you can no longer finesse twice to pick up East's queen to four.

Needing four tricks, the only chance here (**4**) is that the suit breaks 3-3 and the finesse works, so cash the ace then lead low to the jack. Needing only three tricks and being able to afford a loser that would be the wrong play, losing on this layout (**5**).

Looking for three tricks, you should cash the king, then the ace, then lead towards the jack. You get your third trick whenever the suit is 3-3 or West has the queen or when East has queen singleton or doubleton.

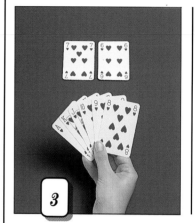

Sometimes, how you should play a suit depends on what contract you are in. Say you are in 7♠ in this situation (**6**). Now you must play spades for no losers. Best is to lead low to the queen and, unless West drops the jack when you go back to dummy to finesse again, cash the ace. Your hope is that East has ♠Kx.

In 6♠ you can afford one loser so can do better. Cash the ace first in case West has a singleton honour. Then cross to dummy to lead towards your queen. What you must avoid is a first-round finesse which loses. How do you know if the distribution is like (**7**) or (**8**), i.e. whether to finesse again or play for

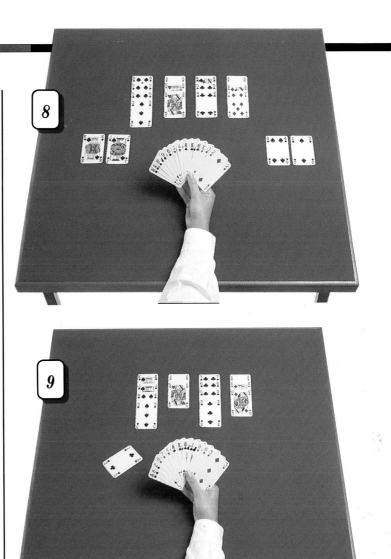

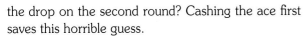

the drop on the second round? Cashing the ace first saves this horrible guess.

How should you play 6NT on a club lead in this situation (**9**)? First, count your tricks – four clubs, three diamonds, two spades and a heart. You need two more and spades must provide at least one of them. You know how to play the spades for four tricks and for three tricks. Which technique do you use?

The key is to take the heart finesse first. If it succeeds you know you need only three spade tricks so play king, ace and low towards the jack. If the heart finesse loses, you need all four spade tricks so play ace then low to the jack (**10**).

AVOIDANCE PLAY

If the title sounds mysterious, don't worry. All it means is that sometimes you get to a position where you know that it is dangerous to lose the lead to one defender, perhaps he has tricks to cash or can attack your weak spot, but perfectly safe to lose the lead to the other defender. Where you have a choice, for example, a two-way finesse for a missing queen, you try to *avoid* losing the lead to the dangerous opponent.

West leads the ◇Q against 4♠ in the next example (**2**). You have at least ten tricks even if you lose to the ♠Q. The only danger is that you might lose three club tricks plus the ♠Q. But this can only happen if East gets in with ♠Q to lead through your ♣K.

East is the dangerous opponent so you should play to avoid her gaining the lead. Win the opening lead and play ♠A then finesse ♠J. If West wins he cannot hurt you as a club lead would be up to your king. Having drawn trumps you can discard a club on the fourth heart to guarantee your contract. Illustration (**3**) shows the complete deal.

In example (**1**) West leads ♣5 against 3NT and East plays the queen. You have eight top tricks and can establish at least one more in spades even if you guess wrongly who has the queen. As you risk giving up the lead, it must be right to try to cut defensive communications. You let ♣Q hold the trick and East plays back ♣10. Again you duck but must win the third club, perforce, throwing a heart from dummy.

The dangerous opponent is West, who surely has the longer clubs if they are not 4-4. Accordingly, cash ♠A and lead ♠J, finessing if West does not play the queen. Even if the finesse loses, East cannot hurt you. If she has a club left to lead, then they must have broken 4-4. The important thing was to avoid giving West the lead.

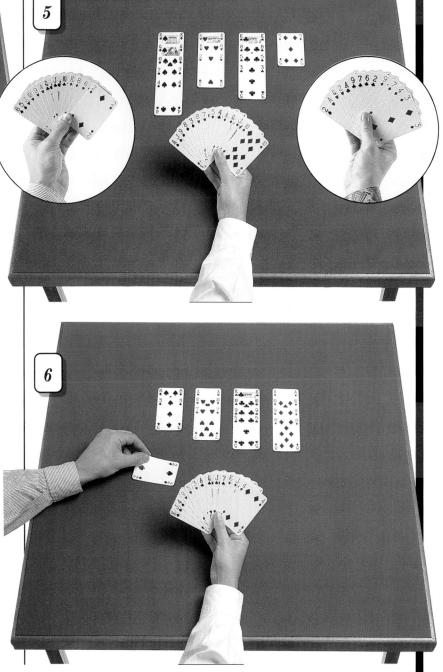

East plays ♠A *then a low spade:* You finesse but West wins the queen and leads a third spade to your king. This time West is the danger hand with spade winners to cash. You play diamonds by cashing the king then finessing the jack. If East wins the queen, either she has no spades or they were 4-4.

On this occasion (**4**) West leads ♣Q against 4♠. You have five trump tricks, ♦A, and can ruff either three clubs in hand or three diamonds in dummy. There are three possibilities for the tenth trick. The ♡A may be with West, you could finesse East for the ♦K, or you could cash ♦A and take the ruffing diamond finesse against West (i.e. cash the ace and lead the queen, and, if West does not cover with the king, discard from dummy). Which is the best play?

Hearts are your weak point as if the ace is offside you could lose three hearts and a club. So West is the dangerous defender, the one who can attack your weakness. Cover the opening lead so he does not get a chance to switch to a heart. Ruff the next club and draw trumps. Now play ♦A and then ♦Q. If the king is not played, throw a heart from dummy. If the queen scores it is your tenth trick, if East wins she can only take one heart trick – she is the safe hand (**5**).

Back to 3NT for this example (**6**) and West leads a low spade. You have a two-way diamond finesse for your contract but can afford to guess wrong, so long as you lose to the safe hand. Which is the safe hand depends on what happens at trick one.

East plays ♠Q: You win the king, play a club to the king and lead ♦10, finessing if East plays low. West is the safe hand as he cannot lead spades effectively, your remaining ♠J4 being a stopper. East, of course, is the danger hand.

BIDDING WITH A PARTSCORE

So far, all your rules for constructive bidding have assumed that you are playing one deal in isolation and that one of the most important decisions you have to make is whether to bid game or to settle for a partscore. In a real life rubber, however, one or both sides might already have a partscore.

As you know, game requires a contract with a trick score of 100 or more. Suppose that you already have a partscore of 40 from the previous deal; now you only need another 60 to bring your total up to game. Take this hand (**1**). Normally, if partner opened 1♡ or 1♠ you would raise him to the three level to invite game. If you already have a partscore of 40, this is a needless risk. 2♡ or 2♠ would give you the extra 60 you need for game without the risk of playing at a level higher and, on a bad day, making only eight tricks to go one down.

This idea should not be carried to excess. If you always bid only to the level required to complete your game, irrespective of your strength, partner will never know whether to look for a slam if he has a strong hand.

I am not suggesting that this is the last word in partscore tactics; after all, you are just starting out in the game and will develop your own ideas as you gain experience. However, for now the following makes reasonable sense.

With a 40 or 60 partscore and partner opens 1♡, what should you bid with the following hands (**2-4**)?

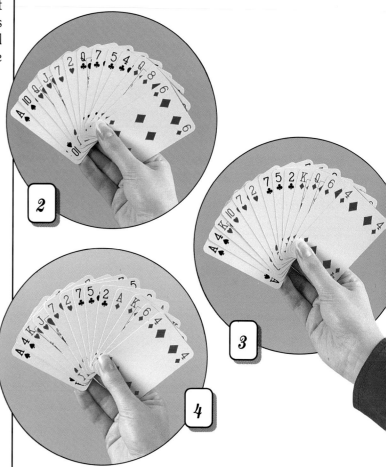

(**2**) Bid only 2♡. You have something to spare but partner would need a huge hand to make a slam while on a bad day eight tricks may be the limit. If an opponent competes with, say, 2♠ you can always bid 3♡.
(**3**) Bid 3♡. This time slam is possible if partner is good, and it would be very unlucky not to make nine tricks.
(**4**) Bid 4♡. Now slam is quite a serious possibility if partner has a little to spare and it is worth the slight risk of only making nine tricks to tell him so.

What the above hands are suggesting is that, apart from raising 1♡ to 2♡ on hands which would always do so, you should raise maybe half a level lower than usual when doing so converts an existing partscore into game. So a poor 3♡ or 4♡ raise should bid only 2♡ or 3♡ respectively, while a very good 3♡ or 4♡ raise makes its normal bid.

NO TRUMP BIDDING

Another area to consider is No Trump bidding. Normally, a 1NT opening bid shows 15-17 HCP. With a 60 partscore, you might stretch this very slightly and open 1NT with:

(i) ♠ Q54   (ii) ♠ KQ9
     ♡ KJ3   ♡ AJ8
     ◇ A1084   ◇ KJ4
     ♣ KJ8   ♣ KJ105

These hands look as though they belong in No Trumps and the odd point is only a small lie. Do not overdo this though or you make it very difficult for partner to know what to do in competition.

With a 30 or 40 partscore your 1NT openings should stick to the normal 15-17 range. If partner raises to 2NT, remember that this is no longer invitational. 2NT scores 70, converting your partscore to game, so you should always pass even with a maximum. In theory, with a partscore of 30 or 40, a raise of 1NT to 3NT is unnecessary so should be invitational to slam. Beware, however, because while this is a good idea, it is sometimes the case that partner has simply forgotten about the partscore. Always try to keep the running score in mind.

Just because you have a partscore should not mean you ignore all the rules of good bidding. The changes suggested above are relatively minor adjustments. What if partner responds in a new suit? You have a 60 partscore and the bidding goes 1♠ – Pass – 2♡ – Pass – ? What should you bid with these hands (**5-7**)?

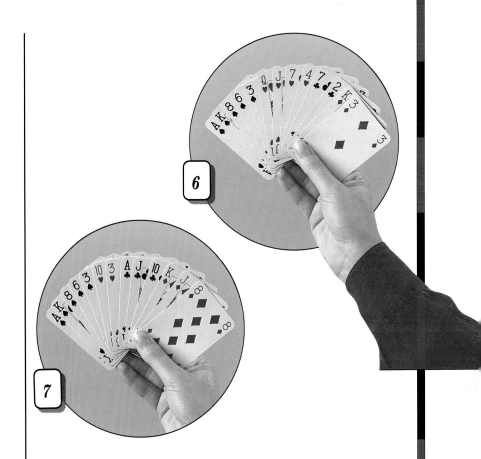

6

7

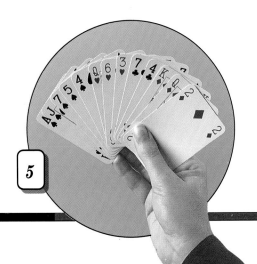

5

(**5**) Pass. You are very minimum and cannot guarantee making 3♡, the bid you would have made without the partscore.

(**6**) 3♡. Now you have a sound opening so should make your normal rebid.

(**7**) 2NT. 2♡ will probably be reasonable, but you have a strong hand so should bid normally.

As responder, you need to be aware that partner may very occasionally pass your change of suit response if that contract is enough for game. It will rarely matter as she will only do so if she is very minimum and has support for your suit. Still, with a very big hand responder can always jump, e.g. 1♠ – 3♡ to make sure opener bids again.

A final thought. Beware opponents who have a partscore. Normally, if your opponents stop bidding at a low level you can be confident that your side has a fair number of high cards and can compete safely. Opponents who have a partscore may have substantial extra values, leaving partner with less than you are hoping for. Be careful only to compete with a reasonable suit as otherwise you could lose some nasty penalties.

ADVANCED BIDDING IDEAS – GAME TRYS

So far we have said that if the bidding begins 1♠ – 2♠ or 1♡ – 2♡ the opener passes with less than 16 points, bids game with 19+ points, and reraises, 1♠ – 2♠ – 3♠ or 1♡ – 2♡ – 3♡, to invite game with 16-18 points.

That is all very well for a complete beginner, but it is quite a cumbersome way of going about things. The problem is that it does not take into account which high cards responder holds. If opener is unbalanced, then some high cards will be much more valuable than others. Give opener and responder the two combinations illustrated (**1**, **2**).

Responding hand (**1**) makes game a near certainty, losing just two aces and perhaps a spade. With hand (**2**), even 3♡ will need some good fortune. If the auction goes 1♡ – 2♡ – 3♡, how is responder to know to bid 4♡ with (**1**) but pass with (**2**)?

Now try it if the auction is 1♡ – 2♡ – 3♣. The first two bids establish that hearts will be trumps, so opener can afford to bid a new suit to help partner to judge how well the two hands fit together and therefore whether to go on to game or settle for 3♡. In our example hand (**1**) bids 4♡ over 3♣ because responder can see that his king and jack of clubs are working overtime. Conversely, three small is a horrible holding in partner's second suit so hand (**2**) should decline the invitation and bid just 3♡.

QUIZ HANDS

Holding the hands illustrated (**3-6**), what should opener rebid after 1♠ – 2♠?

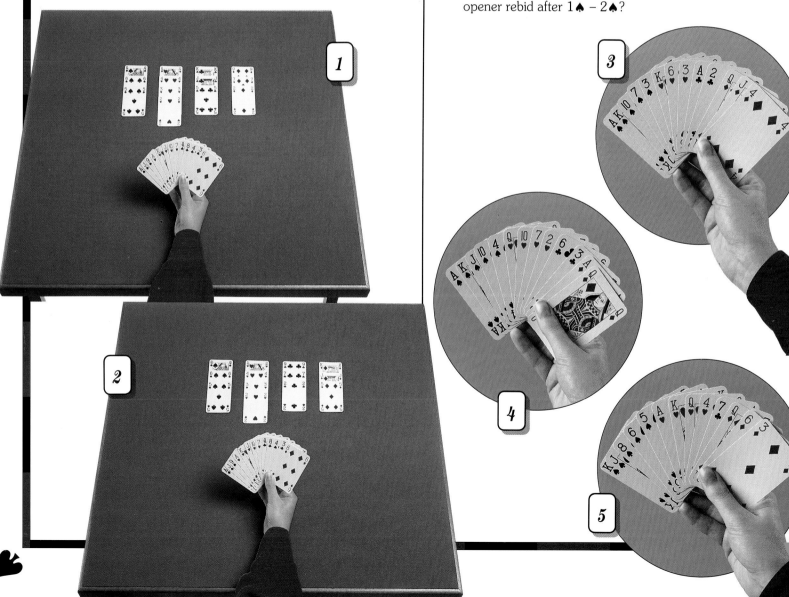

6

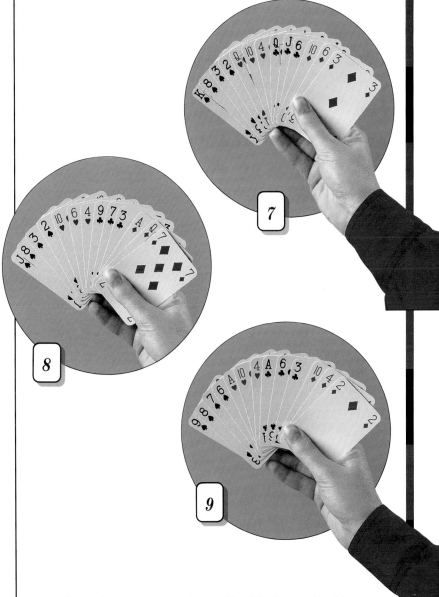

7

8

9

When opener shows a second suit and so is known to be unbalanced, responder should upgrade honours in that suit, counting any ace or king as full value, but downgrade queens and jacks in the unbid suits. So, after 1♠ – 2♠ – 3♢ –?, how would you bid these hands (**7-9**)?

(**3**) Bid 2NT. With a balanced hand, you want partner to value all his high cards equally so describe your hand with a natural bid.

(**4**) Bid 3♡. This time, partner's heart holding could be crucial so bid 3♡ and let partner know to upgrade any heart honours he has.

(**5**) Bid 3♢. 3♡ may look obvious, but it will actually have a negative effect on your chances. Partner cannot have fitting heart honours as you have A, K, Q. He may well have something like three small and think this is bad news, when actually it is just fine. Diamond honours, however, will be much more useful than club honours, except the ace, so 3♢ will help partner more than any alternative.

(**6**) Bid 4♠. No need to invite game when you hold such a good hand.

RESPONDER'S REBID

If opener shows a balanced hand by rebidding 2NT, responder simply bids game with a maximum and goes back to three of the agreed suit with a minimum, so after 1♠ - 2♠ – 2NT – ?, holding this hand

- ♠ Q632
- ♡ J74
- ♢ K85
- ♣ 1096

responder bids 3♠.

- ♠ Q632
- ♡ K74
- ♢ K85
- ♣ J96

With the hand above, responder bids 4♠, or perhaps 3NT to show that responder is also balanced and to give opener a choice of games.

(**7**) is really a minimum, despite the 8 HCP, so should bid 3♠.

(**8**) is a maximum, though it only has 7 HCP, so should jump to 4♠.

(**9**) should bid 4♠, even though there are no top honours in either of opener's suits. Aces are always good cards, whatever suits they may be in.

FOURTH SUIT FORCING (FSF)

The bidding begins 1♡ – 1♠ – 2♣ and responder holds hand (**1**). What should he bid?

1

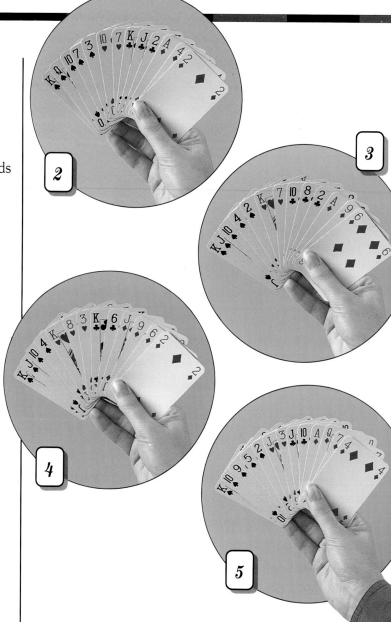

2

3

4

5

You clearly have game values, 13 HCP opposite an opening hand, but can only guess which game. 4♠, 4♡, 5♣ or 3NT could all be right depending on partner's hand – indeed, even 6♣ or 6♠ might make while 3NT might lose the first five tricks. With no known eight-card fit and no stopper in the unbid suit you are in no position to make the final decision.

The solution to this sort of situation is to play a bid of the fourth suit as an artificial bid, asking partner for further information but not necessarily promising any particular holding in the suit bid.

On the example hand you bid 1♡ – 1♠ – 2♣ – 2♢. If opener bids spades you raise to 4♠; if he bids hearts you bid 4♡; if he bids clubs you bid 5♣; if he bids No Trumps you bid 3NT – problem solved.

REQUIREMENTS TO USE FSF

To use FSF (fourth suit forcing) you should have at least invitational values, i.e. about 10/11+ HCP and a desire to know more about partner's hand. Holding the hands illustrated (**2-5**) what would you bid after 1♡ – 1♠ – 2♣ – ?

(**2**) You could just jump to 3NT, but better is 2♢. 3NT may be better played by partner while, if he has a singleton diamond, 4♠, 4♡ or 5♣ could be safer.

(**3**) This time you can only invite game. Again, 2NT is possible, but either hearts or spades may be safer if partner has nothing in diamonds. Bid 2♢ and get some more information.

(**4**) 2♢ would not be a terrible bid but as partner has virtually guaranteed five hearts, a natural invitational bid of 3♡ is best.

(**5**) Bid 2NT, invitational. The reason why you can afford to play FSF is that when you actually have the fourth suit there is rarely any point in bidding it – partner has already shown two suits, after all – just bid No Trumps.

OPENER'S RESPONSE TO FSF

Actually, either player can use FSF, it just happens that responder is far more likely to be the one in a position to use it. If partner uses FSF you should show him the most important feature of your hand that he does not yet know about. In other words, remember your previous bids and see what there is left to tell him about. Consider the following examples (**6-11**).

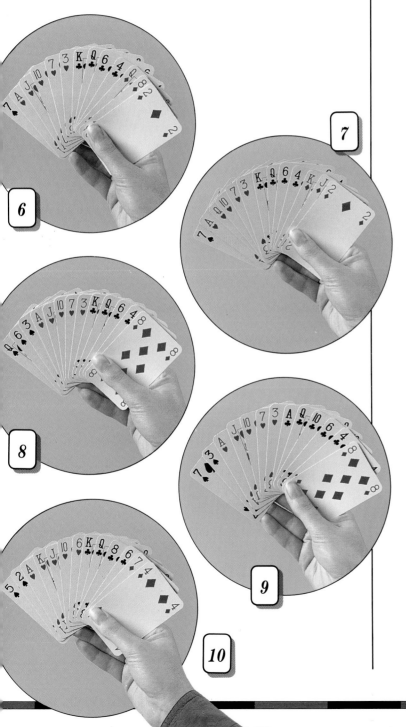

(**6**) Bid 2NT, showing a diamond stopper but a minimum hand. Remember, you already showed five hearts and four clubs.

(**7**) Bid 3NT, showing a diamond stopper and extra values. Partner promised 10+ HCP by bidding the fourth suit so you know you have game values between you.

(**8**) Bid 2♠. You have already denied four-card support so queen to three is quite a significant feature to show.

(**9**) Bid 3♣. So far you have shown five hearts and four clubs. Now show the fifth club.

(**10**) Bid 2♡. You have no extra distributional features to show, nor do you have a diamond stopper. All that is left is to stress the quality of your hearts.

(**11**) Bid 2♠. You would prefer a third spade, but two honours is not bad and with such moderate hearts nothing else appeals.

GENERAL RULES

If the fourth suit is bid at the one or two level it only promises invitational values. If partner's response shows a minimum, it is possible to stop short of game. If partner shows extra values, however, this creates a game force.

FSF at the three level is game forcing. There is no room to stop in a partscore with any confidence.

Bidding the fourth suit then bidding a suit on the next round is forcing, e.g.

1♡ – 1♠
2♣ – 2♢
2NT – 3♡

The same bid without going through FSF would only be invitational, e.g.

1♡ – 1♠
2♣ – 3♡

This allows responder to bid both strong and merely invitational hands intelligently.

SLAM BIDDING

So far we have said that responder should only make a jump bid when he knows where he is going, i.e. when he is making a limit bid in support of opener's suit or in No Trumps. There is no need to jump when responding in a new suit because even a simple change of suit forces partner to bid again, thereby giving you a further chance to describe your hand.

THE JUMP SHIFT

You could survive without ever jumping in a new suit but some very strong hands can be a little awkward to handle if you do not give partner the good news straight away. A jump in a new suit is known as a **jump shift**. Bids such as $1\heartsuit - 2\spadesuit$ and $1\spadesuit - 3\diamondsuit$ show long strong suits and at least 16 HCP or compensating values in the form of an exceptional suit or a fit for partner. They tell partner immediately that game is certain and slam possible and that the bidding must be kept open until game is reached.

Partner opens $1\heartsuit$ and you hold the following hands (**1-3**). What do you bid?

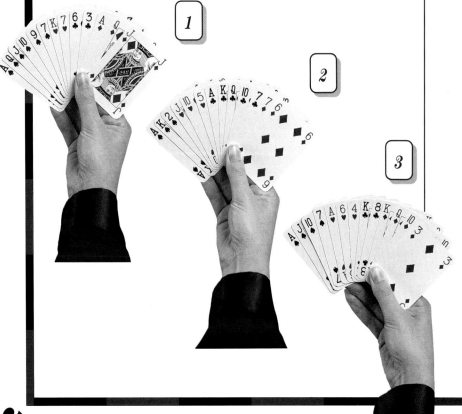

(**1**) This is an ideal hand for a jump shift response of $2\spadesuit$, showing not only the strength of your hand but also a strong suit. Consider what would happen if you responded only $1\spadesuit$ and partner rebid $2\heartsuit$. How would you then continue? You would not wish to give up on spades or on slam possibilities, yet neither $1\heartsuit - 1\spadesuit - 2\heartsuit - 2\spadesuit$ nor $1\heartsuit - 1\spadesuit - 2\heartsuit - 3\spadesuit$ would be forcing. Start with $2\spadesuit$, however, and you can bid a forcing $3\spadesuit$ over any rebid.

(**2**) Again, a jump shift of $3\clubsuit$ is the best start. Slam is a distinct possibility and you have a suit well worth stressing plus 17 HCP. This time, however, you will not repeat the clubs as you have already promised five good ones.

(**3**) Bid $1\spadesuit$. You have the HCP to jump but have no suit worth stressing as a potential trump suit or source of tricks. Bid quietly and hear partner's natural rebid. Not only will this help you to judge the best combined trump suit, it should also give an idea of his strength.

BLACKWOOD

You discover that your side has a good trump fit and considerable strength. Game is certain and slam possible. For slam purposes, counting HCP is not enough; aces and, to a lesser degree, kings become all important.

Say you open $2\clubsuit$ and hear a positive $2\heartsuit$ response. Your hand is as shown in (**4**). If partner holds $\spadesuit76\ \heartsuitA10875\ \diamondsuitA53\ \clubsuit762$, you have 13 top tricks and want to play in 7NT or $7\heartsuit$. He could equally well hold $\spadesuit76\ \heartsuitA10875\ \diamondsuitJ53\ \clubsuitKQ2$, and now there is an inescapable loser – the $\diamondsuit A$ – even though he actually has more HCP.

The solution is the **Blackwood Convention**, named after its inventor, Easley Blackwood. Quite simply, a bid of 4NT, unless the sequence suggests it is natural, asks partner how many aces he has. In response:

$5\clubsuit$ = 0 or 4 aces
$5\diamondsuit$ = 1 ace
$5\heartsuit$ = 2 aces
$5\spadesuit$ = 3 aces

Having asked for aces with 4NT you may then ask for kings in the same way with 5NT. For example; take this bidding sequence:

1♡ –   4♡
4NT(i) –   5◇(ii)
5NT(iii) – 6♡(iv)

(i) Asking for aces
(ii) One ace
(iii) Asking for kings
(iv) Two kings

Blackwood should only be used if you think you have the strength to make a slam as long as two aces are not missing and the answer will solve your problem. Looking at our original example, see how easy it is to find the right contract given responder's two different holdings (**5**, **6**).

(**5**) 2♣ –   2♡
       4NT –   5♡(2 aces)
       7♡/NT – Pass

(**6**) 2♣ – 2♡
       4NT – 5◇(1 ace)
       6♡ – Pass

Here are another couple of examples showing the value of Blackwood (**7**, **8**).

(**7**)   1◇ – 2♠
        3♠ – 4NT
        5♡(i) – 6♠
        Pass
        (i) Two aces

(**8**)   1◇ – 2♠
        3♠ – 4NT
        5◇(i) – 5♠
        Pass
        (i) One ace

SLAM BIDDING – CUEBIDS

While it is a step forward from merely counting HCP, not all potential slam hands are suitable for the use of Blackwood. The problem is that it only tells you *how many* aces and kings partner has, not *which* ones. Sometimes, this can be crucial.

When you have agreed a trump suit and are committed to at least game, there can be no need to bid a new suit in a natural sense. Instead, such a bid can be used to say "partner, I am interested in slam and have a control in this suit, how do you feel about it?" So 1♠ – 3♠ – 4♣ says you have a club control, usually the ace or a void, and slam interest. This is called a **cuebid.** A possible hand might be (**1**). If partner likes his hand he may cuebid in turn. A return to the agreed trump suit is a sign-off, saying you do not like your hand for slam purposes.

Looking at the example hand below, you can see that Blackwood will not necessarily solve your problem as the ♢A is very valuable while the ♡A may be so much waste paper. Responder may hold hand (**2**) or hand (**3**), for example.

Whichever hand responder holds, he will show one ace in response to Blackwood and opener will be guessing. Hand (**3**) makes 13 tricks but hand (**2**) only 11. Cuebidding solves the problem. After 1♠ – 3♠ – 4♣, hand (**2**) bids 4♡, bad news for opener who has no use for the ♡A, while hand (**3**) bids 4♢ – just what opener wanted to hear.

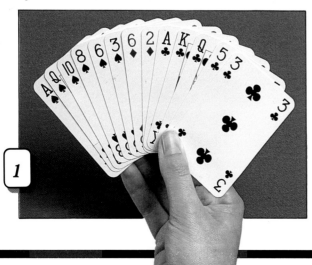

It is permissible to cuebid a second round control (king or singleton) also, but it is normal to do so only after showing all your first round controls. Another rule is that it is normal to bid your cheapest first round control. In other words, if you bypass a suit you deny the control there. For example: 1♠ – 3♠ – 4♢ shows first round diamond control but denies first round club control – the suit bypassed. It follows that:

1♠ – 3♠
4♢ – 4♡
5♣

must show first round diamond control and second round club control.

Let's look at another set of examples (**4**, **5**, **6**).

The auction begins: 2♣ – 2♡
2♠ – 3♠
?

Once more, Blackwood will not help the opener. Her problem is not how many aces responder holds but how many *red* aces. The solution is to cuebid 4♣.

(4) Bids 4♢, showing the ace. Now opener cuebids 5♣ and responder bids 5♡, again showing the ace. Opener can bid 7♠ in complete confidence.

(5) Bids 4♡, showing the ace but denying the ace of diamonds. Knowing one ace is missing, opener settles for 6♠.

(6) Bids 5♣, showing the ace but denying either red ace. Opener settles for a disappointed 5♠.

Compared to Blackwood, cuebidding is a much more delicate and accurate tool. It is also more difficult to use because it requires more judgement from both players. Just because opener cuebids does not mean that responder has to cuebid in turn just because he has an ace. He is allowed to use his judgement of whether his overall hand looks promising for slam. This in turn allows opener to cuebid even when she is not sure about slam even if partner has the missing ace because she knows partner will not show it if the rest of his hand is too poor.

See if you can work out the correct bids on these examples (**7**, **8**, **9**). In each case the auction begins 1♠ – 3♠ and opener cuebids 4♢. What should responder say?

(**7**) Bid 4♡. With two aces, responder should certainly cuebid, particularly as he can do so without raising the level of the bidding. Opener can now cuebid 5♡, pinpointing the club weakness, and responder bids the good slam because of the ♣A.

(**8**) 4♠. Though responder has an ace, the hand is pretty poor with no other ace or king. To cuebid 5♣, above the level of game, should show a good hand. Here, slam is very unlikely if opener cannot bid again over 4♠ (which she will not do on her actual hand).

(**9**) 5♣. Now responder's hand, with an ace and two kings, is very good for his initial 3♠ bid so he should cuebid the ace even though it means going to the five level. Opener will then bid 6♠, confident that the ♡A will be the only loser.

VARIATIONS – THE WEAK NO TRUMP

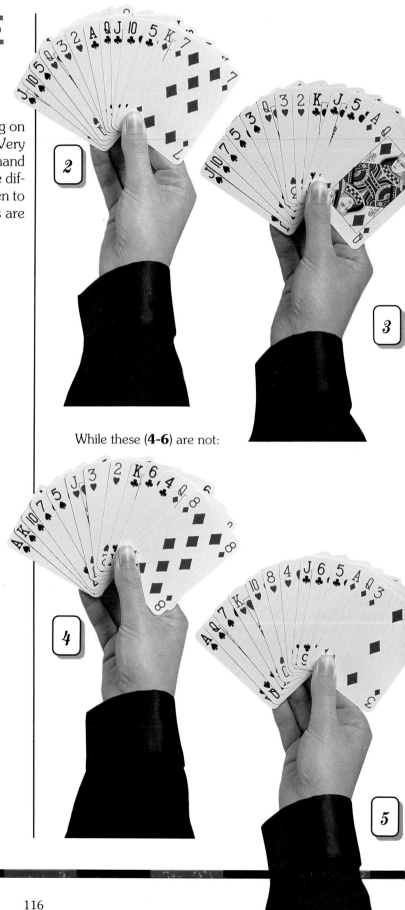

2

3

While these (**4-6**) are not:

4

5

The weak No Trump has been mentioned in passing on more than one occasion in this book. So what is it? Very simply, a weak No Trump opening shows a balanced hand but with 12-14 HCP instead of 15-17. Apart from the difference in strength required, the rules for deciding when to open 1NT and when to open one of a suit or to pass are unchanged.

The weak No Trump is particularly popular in Britain, where it is favoured by a large proportion of tournament players. The standard British bidding system, **Acol**, actually features the variable No Trump, weak when non-vulnerable, strong when vulnerable.

The weak No Trump has both advantages and disadvantages when compared to the strong No Trump. There is the risk of being doubled and conceding a large penalty, hence its use only when non-vulnerable in traditional Acol. Also, it makes it more difficult for the users to reach the right partscore contracts when the opener has a balanced minimum opener. Against that, it pre-empts the opposition out of their partscores on occasions. Its biggest advantage is, however, that when opener bids one of a suit he is known to have extra values either in terms of extra high cards or in terms of distribution. As you gain in experience you will see that this can be very helpful, particularly in competitive auctions.

These examples (**1-3**) are all suitable for a weak No Trump opening:

1

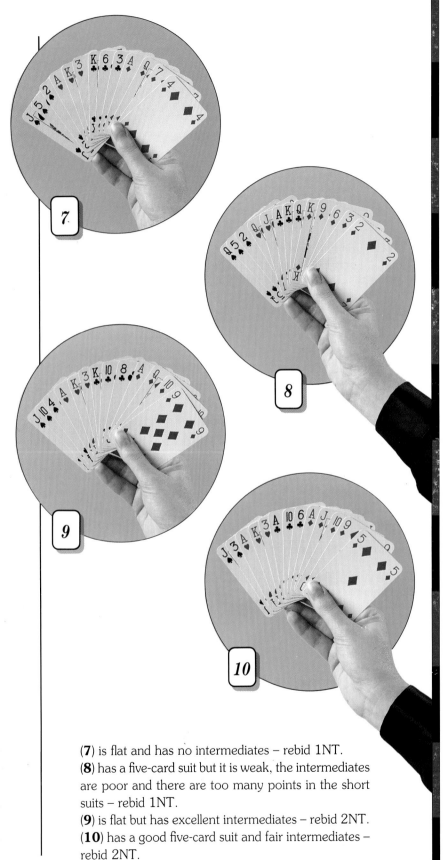

(**4**) is a 1♠ opener. A weak five-card major can be opened 1NT, or any five-card minor, but a hand with a strong five-card major should open the major and usually rebid it.

(**5**) is a strong No Trump opener. This hand is too strong for 1NT and should open 1♡.

(**6**) Though the strength is right, 5-4-2-2 is not a No Trump shape. This hand should open 1◇, intending to rebid 2♣ over a 1♡/♠ response.

We have been used to opening 1NT with 15-17 HCP and opening one of a suit then rebidding No Trumps with a balanced 12-14 HCP. Playing the weak No Trump, No Trump rebids are as follows:

```
1◇ – 1♠ – 1NT = 15-17
        – 2NT = 17-18
        – 3NT = 19-20
1◇ – 2♣ – 2NT = 15-17
        – 3NT = 17-20
```

As you see, we have simply swapped things round. 17 points is the borderline where you can either make a simple or a jump rebid. A good 17, one with a five-card suit or lots of tens and nines, should jump, while a poor 17, very flat or lacking in intermediates should make the simple rebid.

After 1◇ – 1♠, how would you bid with these hands (**7-10**)?

(**7**) is flat and has no intermediates – rebid 1NT.

(**8**) has a five-card suit but it is weak, the intermediates are poor and there are too many points in the short suits – rebid 1NT.

(**9**) is flat but has excellent intermediates – rebid 2NT.

(**10**) has a good five-card suit and fair intermediates – rebid 2NT.

VARIATIONS – FIVE-CARD MAJORS

A very popular agreement is to play that an opening bid of one of a major promises at least a five-card suit. This can help with constructive bidding as it gives a very sound basis for the subsequent auction, but it is most valuable in competition as responder can afford to support opener's suit much more readily than when possibly facing a four-card suit.

There is one obvious problem, of course: what to open with a balanced hand outside the opening No Trump range and with no five-card major. The answer is to open one of your longer minor suit, even though it may be less than four cards in length. With 3-3 in the minors, open 1♣, so that the only time it is necessary to open 1♢ with less than four is if you have precisely 4♠-4♡-3♢-2♣.

Assuming five-card majors and a strong No Trump, what should you open with the following hands (**1-3**)?

(**1**) 1♣, just as you would have done if playing four-card majors.

(**2**) 1♣. Though the diamonds are stronger, with equal length in the minors prefer 1♣, that way partner can support diamonds more confidently knowing that you will nearly always hold four when you open 1♢.

(**3**) 1♢. This is the one time you have to open a three-card diamond suit, when you only have a doubleton club.

PARTNER OPENS 1♡/♠

You can afford to raise a one of a major opening anytime you have three-card support, though a very flat hand may occasionally prefer not to raise immediately. So, in these examples (**4-7**), how would you reply to an opening bid of 1♡?

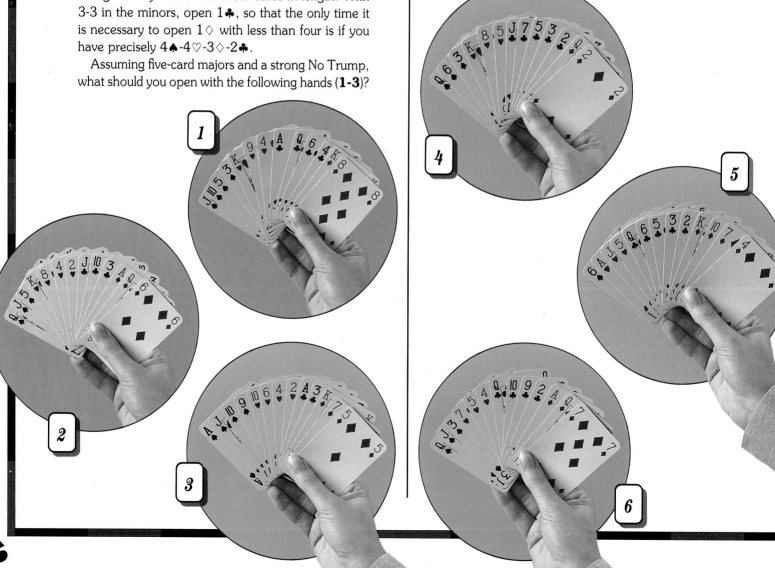

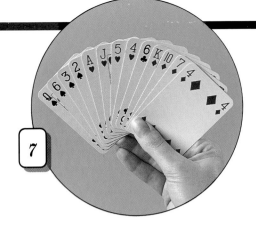

7

(**4**) would have bid 1NT opposite a four-card 1♡ opening but now can raise immediately to 2♡, knowing of an eight-card fit.

(**5**) would bid 2♣ over a four-card 1♡ opening but now can raise to 3♡ with good three-card support and a ruffing value.

(**6**) would bid 2NT over a four-card 1♡ opening and should still do so. The hand is completely flat, the hearts are weak and you have a sure stopper in every other suit.

(**7**) would bid only 3♡ over a four-card 1♡ opening, but knowing of at least a nine-card fit a raise directly to 4♡ is a reasonable shot.

PARTNER OPENS 1♣/◇

You can afford to raise diamonds almost as freely as usual but need to be a little wary of raising clubs if there is any alternative. Even with good support for partner's minor you should bid a four-card major if you have one, in case you also have a fit there. Again, consider these examples (**8, 9**) and decide how you would reply to 1◇.

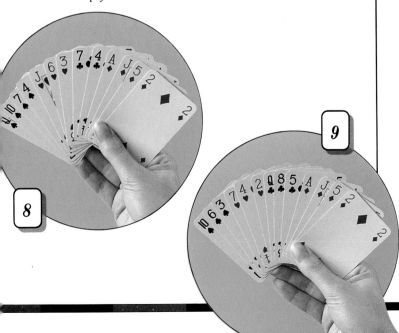

9

8

(**8**) Bid 1♠, checking for the major suit fit. You can always support diamonds next time.

(**9**) Raise to 2◇. Not only do you have four-card support but most of your strength is in partner's suit.

In the next examples (**10, 11**), how would you reply to 1♣?

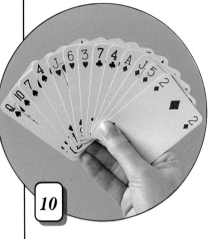

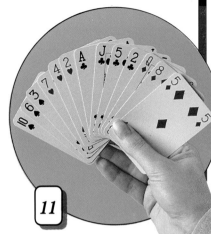

10

11

(**10**) Bid 1♠. You only intend to bid one of your suits and the major suit fit is far more important than diamonds,

(**11**) Bid 1NT. Compare this with example (**9**). The difference is that 1♣ will be only a three-card suit far more often than 1◇, making it advisable to raise only as a last resort.

OPENER REBIDS

One advantage of five-card majors is that a minimum balanced hand opens one of a minor so you avoid sequences like 1♠ – 2♣ – 2NT on flat 12 counts. With the one exception of 1◇ – 2♣ – 2NT, all weak No Trump types get to rebid 1NT – much more comfortable. I believe it is very important to tell partner what type of hand you have – balanced or unbalanced – as soon as possible so, unless responder bids his four-card suit, opener should rebid 1NT with a balanced 12-14 rather than bid a second suit at the one level. For example:

♠ Q1074
♡ K4
◇ QJ8
♣ AJ63

After 1♣ – 1◇/♡ – ?, prefer to rebid 1NT rather than 1♠, thereby giving partner a good picture of your strength and shape.

VARIATIONS – WEAK TWO BIDS

We saw earlier how difficult it can be to handle our opponents' pre-emptive openings at the three level and higher. Many players, particularly in the tournament world, want to be able to pre-empt even more often. As strong two openings are comparatively rare, they use opening bids of 2♡ and 2♠ (some also use 2◇) as mini-pre-empts, showing a six-card suit and about 6-10 HCP.

Typical examples would be hands **1** and **2**.

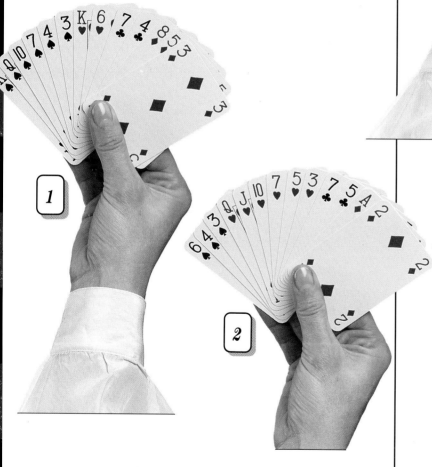

These next two examples (**3**, **4**) would not be suitable for most players. In (**3**) the suit is very weak and you have a lot of defensive values outside it. To open 2♠ could lead to a silly contract and will make it very tough for partner to judge correctly.

The suit is reasonable in (**4**), but having a good four-card holding in the other major is a serious flaw. If you open 2♠ there is too big a risk of pre-empting your own side out of a good contract in hearts.

PARTNER OPENS 2♡/♠ (WEAK)

You want to make life as difficult as possible for your opponents, so a direct raise of partner's suit is best played as not being constructive, merely continuing the pre-empt. Just as opposite a weak three opening, a change of suit is natural and forcing for one round, while a 2NT response is completely artificial and is the way to start if you are interested in game. There are many schemes available for responding to the 2NT enquiry bid. Here is one of the most popular:

2♠ – 2NT – 3♣ = minimum (6-8) with a poor suit
  – 3◇ = minimum with a good suit (at least AJ10xxx or two of the top three honours)
  – 3♡ = maximum (8-10) but a poor suit
  – 3♠ = maximum with a good suit
  – 3NT = AKQxxx

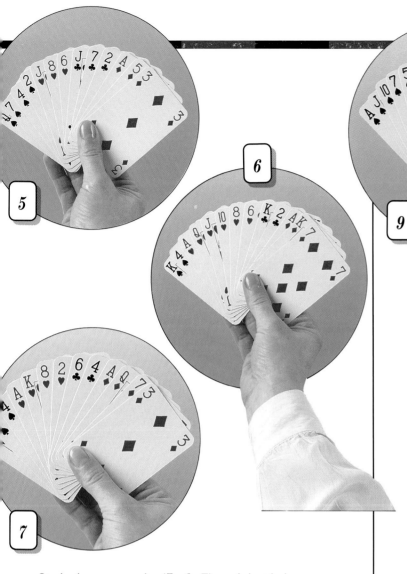

(8) Bid 3♡, showing a maximum but a poor suit.
(9) Bid 3◇, a minimum but a good suit.
(10) Bid 3♠, maximum plus a good suit.

STRONG HANDS

If you play weak two openings you need some way of showing hands which would normally open with a strong two bid. The most convenient scheme is to use a 2◇ opening to show the very big hand which is normally opened 2♣, and play 2◇ – 2♡ as the negative response. After that, the bidding goes exactly as after a 2♣ opening playing traditional methods.

That leaves a 2♣ opening to show the eight/nine playing trick hand in any suit. Responder bids 2◇ unless he has a very good suit of his own to show and then opener bids his suit. So:

2♣ – 2◇ = neutral, not necessarily a negative
2♣ – 2♡ etc = A positive with a good suit
2♣ – 2◇ – 2♡/♠/3♣/◇ = A strong two opening in the bid suit.

After which the bidding follows the same rules as if you had opened a strong two bid in the first place.

This scheme also allows you to show very strong balanced hands more accurately than usual.
2NT = 20-21
2♣ then rebid 2NT = 22-23
2◇ then rebid 2NT = 24-25
2♣ then rebid 3NT = 26-27
2◇ then rebid 3NT = 28-29

Study these examples (**5, 6, 7**), and decide how you would reply to partner's opening bid of 2♠.
(**5**) Raise to 3♠, pre-emptively. This does not invite partner to bid again.
(**6**) Bid 3♡, natural and forcing. Partner will raise with three small or honour doubleton.
(**7**) Bid 2NT, asking partner about his hand. You are interested in game if partner has a maximum.

Now put yourself in opener's position and work out your rebid after the auction has begun 2♠ – 2NT – ?, holding these hands (**8, 9** and **10**).

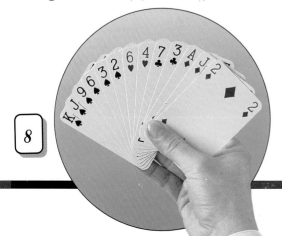

ETHICS AND ETIQUETTE

Bridge is many things to many people but above all else it is a game played for enjoyment. One should always try to remember this and remain pleasant to partners, however stupid their last bid or play seems to have been. Whatever one might think at times, partner is trying to do the right thing and perhaps he or she had a more difficult decision than is evident from our side of the table. To be critical not only spoils partner's enjoyment of the game but is also likely to have a negative effect on his or her future performance.

Likewise, one should always be polite to opponents. They may be the opposite side in the game but they should not be thought of as the enemy. Treat them as you would wish to be treated and everyone can have a pleasant, albeit competitive, game.

Very few people go into a game of bridge intent on cheating, but it is a game at which it is possible to cheat unintentionally. The important thing to remember is that the information you are entitled to use from your partner is the bids and plays he makes, not *the way* he makes them.

If you make an opening lead and notice partner smile or frown, it is not difficult to guess whether he likes your lead. Similarly, a quick bid suggests an automatic decision, a slow bid a close decision. The most obvious example is a slow Pass, clearly suggesting a hand nearly worth a bid.

In all cases, the ethical thing to do is to bend over backwards not to take advantage of partner's body language or tempo. You will be a more popular and respected player if you do the opposite of what this illicit information suggests will be successful, whenever you have a plausible alternative. What is more, you will feel better about yourself.

GLOSSARY

Acol The standard domestic Bidding System in Great Britain

Attitude signal When partner leads a suit and you do not need to play a high card to try to win the trick, to follow with a high spot card encourages partner to continue the suit, a low spot card discourages.

Auction The sequence of bids

Balanced Hand A flat hand, one with no very long or short suits

Blackwood An artificial 4NT bid asking partner for aces

Conventional bid Any artificial bid, for example Blackwood or Stayman

Count signal When following suit with small cards, to play high-low shows an even number of cards in the suit, low-high an odd number.

Cross-ruff To play the hand by repeatedly ruffing two suits in alternation, one in dummy, one in your own hand.

Cuebid An artificial bid. Either showing a control card in a slam auction, or simply forcing if bid in the opponents' suit

Declarer The player who plays the contract

Defenders Declarer's opponents

Discard To throw away a card when unable to follow suit and either unwilling or unable to ruff

Double A bid which, if it ends the auction, increases the score for the successful side

Doubleton Any suit of precisely two cards

Draw trumps To lead trumps until your opponents are exhausted of the suit

Duck To play a low card when holding a higher one which might win the trick

Dummy Declarer's partner

Echo Sometimes called a peter. To play high-low with two small cards in defence as a signal to partner. Usually this either encourages the suit or shows an even number of cards in it

Entry A way of getting into a particular hand

Finesse An attempt to win a trick with a card which is lower than at least one held by your opponents

Fit Your side's combined holding in a suit

Follow suit To play a card in the same suit as the card led to the trick – a requirement of the laws whenever possible

Forcing bid A bid which partner is not allowed to Pass

Game A contract with a trick score of 100 points or more

Game forcing A bid which says that your partnership must keep bidding until game is reached

Grand slam A contract which requires declarer to take all 13 tricks, but which gives a large bonus score if successful

Hand A player's 13 cards; sometimes used instead of deal, e.g. "We played sixteen deals/hands last night"

HCP High Card Points

Honours The AKQJ10 of a suit. Bonus points can be scored for holding at least four of the trump honours in the same hand, or all four aces in a No Trump contract

Invitational A bid which is not forcing but which encourages partner to bid on if he has above minimum values

Jump bid Any bid where the same suit could have been bid legally at a lower level

Jump overcall To overcall at a level one higher than necessary to show your suit (e.g. 1♥ – 3♣). This shows a good six-card suit and a good opening hand

Jump shift To jump in a new suit in response to partner's bid (e.g. 1♦ – 2♠). This shows a strong suit and a strong hand

Lead The first card played to a trick

Limit bid A bid showing the strength of your hand within a narrow range. Normally, partner is allowed to Pass a limit bid

No bid Another way of saying Pass

Non-forcing bid A bid from partner which you are allowed to Pass

Non-vulnerable The situation before your side has scored a game in the rubber

Overcall A bid in a new suit or No Trumps after an opponent has opened the bidding

Overtrick An extra trick above the number needed to fulfil your contract

Partscore A contract with a trick value of less than 100. Also an existing score towards game

Pass What you say when you do not wish to make a positive bid

Penalty The score conceded when you fail to fulfil your contract

Penalty double A double intended to end the auction and which increases the score for the successful side

Peter Sometimes called an echo. To play high-low with two small cards in defence as a signal to partner. Usually either encourages the suit or shows an even number of cards in it.

Point count A way of judging the strength of your hand, giving an artificial value to each honour card in your hand

Pre-empt A jump bid based on a long suit rather than high card strength

Redouble A bid which increases the score even further after a double

Reverse A strong bid when a new suit bid raises the level of the auction above the next level of your first suit

Revoke To fail to follow suit when able to do so

Rubber The best of three games

Ruff To trump

Rule of eleven A way of deducing declarer's holding in a suit assuming partner has led his fourth-best card

Sequence A run of two or more touching honour cards

Signal To play a card in defence which gives a special message to partner

Singleton A suit of precisely one card

Small slam A contract which requires declarer to make 12 tricks to succeed. There are large bonuses for successfully bidding and making a small slam

Standard American The most popular Bidding System in the USA

Stayman An artificial response of 2♣ to 1NT or 3♣ to 2NT, asking partner to bid a four-card major suit

Stopper A holding in a suit which prevents your opponents running the suit without your gaining the lead

Support Your holding in a suit bid by partner

Takeout double An artificial double which asks partner to bid

Tenace A holding of two honour cards that are not in sequence, e.g. AQ

Trick The play of one card from each player

Trump A special master suit decided during the auction. Also to play a trump when another suit was led to the trick; this is also known as a ruff

Unblock To play the high cards from the short hand first so as to be able to cash the winners in the long hand later

Undertrick A trick less than the number required to make your contract

Void A suit with no cards in it

Vulnerable The situation after you have won a game in the rubber

SCORING TABLE

Below the line

Trick score
For each trick over six bid and made:

	UNDOUBLED	DOUBLED	REDOUBLED
In clubs or diamonds	20	40	80
In hearts or spades	30	60	120
In No Trumps (first trick)	40	80	160
(each subsequent trick)	30	60	120

The first side to score 100 points below the line wins a game and is said to be vulnerable. Both sides start from scratch for the next game. The first side to win two games wins the rubber.

Above the line

Bonuses
For honours in one hand
All five trump honours, or four aces at No Trumps – 150
Four trump honours – 100

For bidding and making a slam	NOT VULNERABLE	VULNERABLE
Small slam (12 tricks)	500	750
Grand slam (13 tricks)	1000	1500

For winning the rubber	**Unfinished rubber**
In two games – 700	One game in unfinished rubber – 300
In three games – 500	A part-score in unfinished game – 100

For making any doubled contract – 50
For making any redoubled contract – 100

Overtricks

For each overtrick made:	UNDOUBLED	DOUBLED	REDOUBLED
Not vulnerable	Trick value	100	200
Vulnerable	Trick value	200	400

Undertricks
Penalties scored by defenders when declarer falls short of contract.

	UNDOUBLED	DOUBLED		REDOUBLED	
	Each Trick	First Trick	Subsequent Tricks	First Trick	Subsequent Tricks
Not vulnerable	50	100	200	200	400
Bonus for 4th and each subsequent undertrick	0	100		200	
Vulnerable	100	200	300	400	600

BIDDING SUMMARY

This is a summary of the standard domestic bidding systems in Great Britain and the USA. The system used in this book is based on British Acol but is sufficiently close to Standard American that there should be no difficulty in making the minor adjustments required to use it in either country. (NV = Non-Vulnerable, V = Vulnerable)

OPENING BID	ACOL	STANDARD AMERICAN
1NT	Traditionally variable, 12-14 NV, 15-17 V. Many people now play one range throughout. Balanced, i.e. 4-3-3-3, 4-4-3-2 or 5-3-3-2.	By agreement, either 15-17 or 16-18 throughout. Balanced.
1♣/1♦/1♡/1♠	12-20 points. Longest suit first. With 4-4, bid the lower ranking suit; with 5-5 the higher – except 1♣ with five clubs and five spades.	12-21 points.
2NT	Balanced 20-22.	Balanced 22-24.
2♦/2♡/2♠	One round force; 8+ sure winners, 16+ points and at least a five-card suit.	Game forcing; 9+ tricks or 22+ points and at least a five-card suit.
2♣	Artificial, usually game forcing. 23+ points or 10+ tricks.	Traditionally, natural and game forcing. Sometimes played as in Acol.
3♣/3♦/3♡/3♠	Pre-emptive. Normally a good seven-card suit but little else. Insufficient high cards for a one level opening. Usually about 6 playing tricks NV, 7 playing tricks V.	
3NT	A solid seven or eight-card minor and little else – by agreement, at most a king or denying a king.	Balanced 25-27.
4♣/4♦/4♡/4♠	Similar to a three level opening but with one extra playing trick. 4♡/4♠ may sometimes have the high card strength for a one level opening.	

VARIATIONS	ACOL	STANDARD AMERICAN
5-Card Majors	Becoming more popular but still quite rare	1♡/1♠ promise five cards. With only a four-card major, open the longer minor even if only three cards. 1♣ with 3-3 in minors
Weak Two Bids	2♦/2♡/2♠ show six-card suits and less than an opening bid. Usually 6-10 HCP in Acol	The range varies; both 6-10 and 8-12 are popular. 2♣ now has to be the Acol-style artificial game force.

RESPONSES	ACOL	STANDARD AMERICAN
To 1NT	2♣ is Stayman, asking for a four-card major. 2♦/2♡/2♠ are weak with a five+ card suit. 3♣/3♦/3♡/3♠ are strong, forcing to game with a five+ card suit. Any game or slam bid is to play. A 2NT raise invites game. Opposite a 15-17 No Trump it shows around 9 HCP, opposite a 12-14 it would show 11-12 HCP. A 4NT raise invites slam. It shows about 16-17 HCP opposite a 15-17 No Trump; 19-20 opposite 12-14.	
To 1♣/1♦/1♡/1♠	With 0-5 points, Pass. With 6-9, give a simple raise, bid 1NT, or a new suit at the one-level. With 10-12, give a jump raise to the three level, bid 2NT, or bid a new suit at either the one or two level. With 13+ raise to game, bid 3NT, or bid a new suit at the one or two level. All bids in a new suit are forcing for one round. 1♠–2♡ promises five cards.	
Jump Shift	16+ points and a good suit; game forcing.	18+ points and a good suit; game forcing.
To 2NT	3♣ is Stayman, asking for a four-card major. 3♦/3♡/3♠ are game forcing with at least a five-card suit. Game and slam bids are all to play. 4NT invites slam.	
To Natural Strong Twos	2NT is a negative (0-7 HCP). All other bids show 8+ and are game forcing. A simple raise will usually include at least one ace, while a jump raise will deny one. A new suit promises five+ cards.	

RESPONSES	ACOL and STANDARD AMERICAN
To An Artificial 2♣	2♦ is a negative (0-7 HCP). All other bids show 8+ and are game forcing. A new suit is usually five+ cards though a strong four-card suit may be shown at the two level.
To Weak Twos	Raises are not constructive; i.e. opener is supposed to Pass. A game raise can be two way, either pre-emptive or hoping to make game. A new suit is natural and forcing – usually a long, strong suit. 2NT is a strong artificial enquiry.
To Three Openings	With no fit, usually Pass unless very strong. Any game bid is to play. Raises may be two way – pre-emptive or strong. A new suit bid is natural and forcing with a long, strong suit.

OPENER'S REBID	ACOL and STANDARD AMERICAN
In Own Suit	A simple rebid (e.g. 1♡–1♠–2♡) shows at least a five-card suit and 12-15 points. A jump rebid (e.g. 1♡–1♠–3♡) is highly invitational, showing 16-18 points and at least a six-card suit.
In No Trumps	If playing a 15-17 No Trump opening, a 1NT rebid show 12-14 HCP, balanced, as does 2NT after a two over one response. A jump to 2NT shows 17-18. A 3NT jump after a one level response shows 19-20 (in Standard American, 19-21), and after a two level response 17-20 (17-21).
In Partner's Suit	A simple raise shows 12-15, usually with four-card support though three cards are permitted. A jump raise shows 16-18 with four-card support. A game raise shows 19-20 with four-card support. None of these raises is forcing.
In a New Suit	A new suit at the lowest available level and below the next level of opener's first suit shows 12+ points and four+ cards. A jump in a new suit shows 17+ points and is game forcing. A reverse, bidding a new suit at the lowest available level but above the next level of opener's first suit (e.g. 1♡–2♣–2♠), show 16+ points, guarantees five+ cards in the first suit and, if the response was at the two level, is game forcing.

OVERCALLS	ACOL and STANDARD AMERICAN
Simple Suit Bid	At least a five-card suit. At the one level about 8-15 HCP, at the two level 11-15.
Jump Suit Bid	At least a good six-card suit, around 12-16 HCP.

OVERCALLS	ACOL and STANDARD AMERICAN
Double Jump In A Suit	Pre-emptive; similar to opening with the same bid.
1NT	By agreement, either 15-17 or 16-18 balanced. Guarantees a sure stopper in the opponents' suit. Also, by agreement, can be played as weaker in the pass-out seat, e.g. 11-14.

CONVENTIONS	ACOL and STANDARD AMERICAN
Stayman	A 2♣ response to a 1NT opening is artificial. It asks opener to bid a four-card major. With no major he rebids 2♦; with both majors 2♡.
Blackwood	Unless clearly a natural bid, 4NT asks partner for his number of aces. Standard responses are 5♣ (0 or 4); 5♦ (1); 5♡ (2); 5♠ (3). After using 4NT, the same player may bid 5NT to ask for kings with equivalent responses.
Cuebids	Where a trump suit is clearly agreed, a bid in a new suit which commits the bidder to at least game is a slam try, showing a control in the bid suit. Usually this is the ace or a void, though a king or singleton is permitted.
Game Try	Where a trump suit is clearly agreed, a new suit bid which does not commit the bidder to game is a game try in the agreed suit. It usually shows three+ cards in the second suit and asks partner for help in the suit.
Fourth Suit Forcing	A bid of the fourth suit, all by the same side, is not natural but shows at least invitational values and asks partner to describe his hand further.
Takeout Double	A double of an opposing suit bid, if the doubling side's first positive call in the auction, is for take out. It show opening strength and support for the unbid suits and asks partner to bid.
Directional Asking Bid	A bid of the opponents' suit, other than where clearly a slam try cuebid, is game forcing and asks partner to describe his hand, with particular reference to a stopper in the opponents' suit for No Trump purposes.